Stock Market Investing For Beginners 2022

The Complete and Quick Guide to Becoming a Millionaire Investor. Learn How to Build and Diversify Your Investment Portfolio and Your Wealth. Bonus Indicators Included.

John De Vecchi

IPH BOOKS

Thanks to trading you are free. It is possible to live and work anywhere in the world. You can be independent of the routine and answer to nobody.

With this book, I want to invite you to consider, even in the darkest times, what trading and investments give: freedom.

Put effort, passion, and the right mindset and all this will become reality as it has become for me.

Enjoy reading

John De Vecchi

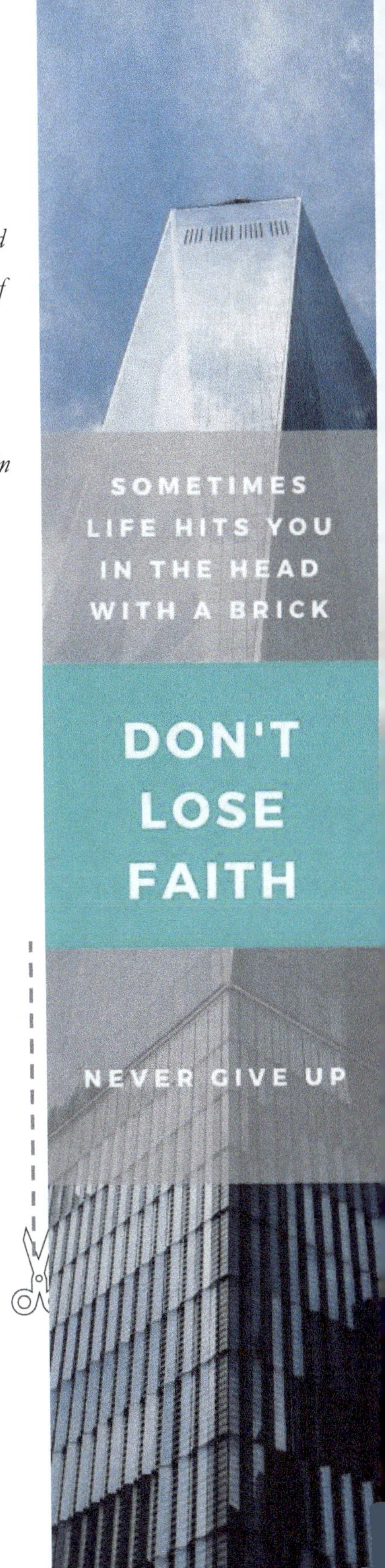

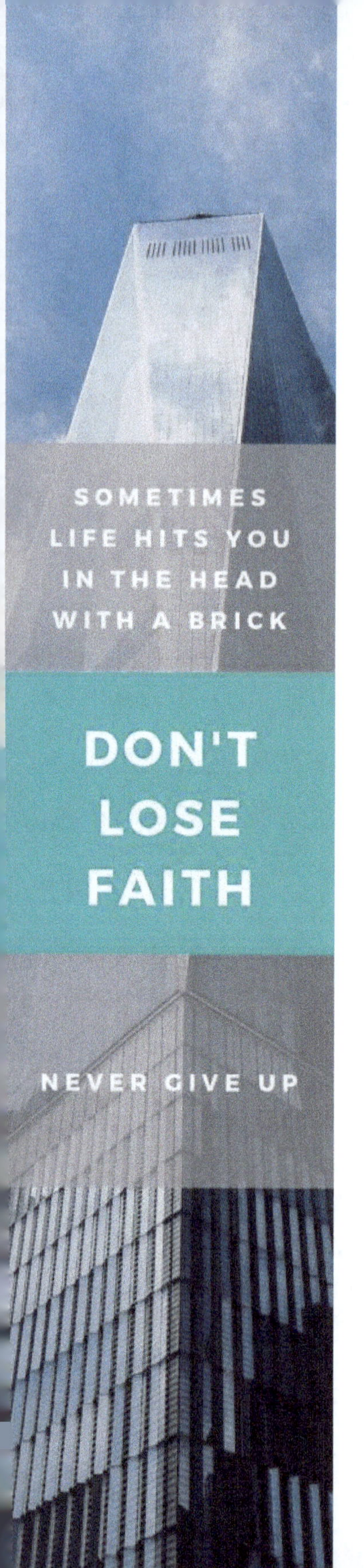

SOMETIMES
LIFE HITS YOU
IN THE HEAD
WITH A BRICK
DON'T
LOSE
FAITH
NEVER GIVE UP

Table of Content

The stock market is the place investors associate with buy and sell investments, usually stocks, which are shares of proprietorship in an open organization. Stocks, otherwise called values, speak to fragmentary proprietorship in an organization, and the stock market is where investors can buy and sell responsibility for investible resources.

A stock market considered monetary advancement as it enables companies to get to capital from the general population rapidly. It is where shares of pubic recorded companies are exchanged. The essential market is the place companies glide shares to the overall population in the first sale of stock to raise capital.

Different elements go into the choices of traders and investors about where to buy and sell singular stocks. The most significant is the profitability of the organization, as well as its possibilities for profits. Traders are continually looking for advances.

They use past value activity as charts to illuminate their choices to sell or buy; however, whether they settle or not on the transaction depends on the events that will occur

Most beginners—investors and traders—have quite confused ideas when approaching the stock market, investing in stocks (or options, ETFs, commodities, etc.) or trading in general. One of the pivotal points that creates confusion in those interested in making their money work through investments is the lack of understanding of the crucial difference between trading and investing.

The confusion derives from the fact that in the eyes of the investor or the uneducated and non-conscious trader, doing trading or investing seems to be the same thing.

Although they are united by the desire to make a profit, the two operations arise from different logic and follow different rules. Those who invest measure the value of what they buy (an action, a house, a business, an object of art, etc.), try to buy it at a discounted or otherwise balanced price.

The entire operation is based on the prediction or hope that, over time, the good purchased will increase in value and that this increase in value will automatically be reflected in a corresponding rise in its market price, allowing it to be sold for a profit.

An easily understandable example of investment is that of those who buy agricultural land in the expectation that it will then be buildable. The greatest investors of history, such as the legendary Warren Buffett, are, in fact, masters in buying "depreciated quality." Of course, their time horizon is never very short, and the value of what they have purchased can remain or even go down for a specified period without this causing them to worry excessively.

Trades, however, do not bet on a change in the value of things. The hard and pure trader does not care highly about the objective quality or the nature of what he buys and only interested in acquiring it at a price in a short time frame he plans to grow, even though the value of what he purchased remains perfectly identical.

What makes trading possible is that the prices of things and, therefore also investment objects such as shares, bonds, real estate, etc. may vary regardless of their value due to the law of supply and offer.

The stock market fills two significant needs. The first is to give money to companies that they can use to fund and grow their organizations. If an organization issues one million shares of stock that at the first sell for $10 an offer, at that point that furnishes the organization with $10 million of capital that it can use to develop its business less whatever expenses the organization pays for an investment bank to deal with the stock contribution.

By offering stock shares as opposed to getting the capital required for an extension, the organization abstains from bringing about obligation and paying interest charges on that obligation. The optional reason the stock market serves is to give investors, the individuals who buy stocks, a chance to partake in the profits of traded on an open market company.

The stock market empowers buyers and sellers to arrange costs and make exchanges.

Investors would then be able to buy and sell these stocks among themselves, and the exchange tracks the organic market of each recorded stock. It helps decide the cost for every security or the levels at which stock market members, investors, and traders are happy to buy or sell.

Chapter 1.

How to Get Started?

Topic Covered:

♦ Planning and Meeting Goals

♦ Choosing an Investment Method

♦ Choosing a Stockbroker

♦ Opening an Account

♦ Buying and Selling Stocks

Stock may seem incredibly intimidating for those starting in the investment world. It looks like a completely different world, and the hardest step for most is the beginning. However, it is quite simple to get started in stock investments. First, one must set goals for ourselves and determine how we would like to invest in stocks. By writing down goals and ensuring that the investor's money is used in the best possible way, the trader is helping them yield the highest return on their investment. Once the individual's goals are made clear, they must plan on how to meet those goals. Then, it must be decided where exactly the investor will invest their money. It is crucial, as this will be the platform in which they will trade their stocks. After this, the investor must open an account with whomever they choose and deposit an initial amount. While doing so, they may have to link their bank account to their stock trading account. The investor may then begin the process of buying and selling. Although this seems like a lengthy process, it is quite simple.

Planning and Meeting Goals

Ever since the investor must familiarize themselves with their goals, it is quite helpful to write them down in each area and put them in an easily accessible place. It is obligatory to have measurable goals to reach. This way, there may be a specific period and amount that may be assigned to the targets. It may help to come up with monthly goals. For instance, the investor may start with the purchase of 100 shares of stock in February and increase that to 150 shares by March, 200 shares by April, and so on. This way, the investor may have a period to achieve their goals and measure the progress easily. To set proper goals, one must reflect upon our limits and needs. How much will the investor be able to set aside for stock realistically? If one's goals are not realistic, it may become discouraging and set the investor back from their full potential. At the time of trading, the investor must consider any past investments they have made. They must consider what worked and what did not. It is crucial to take into account income and expenses, and also any savings goals they may have. This will make it more clear what may be invested in stocks.

Without a clear guide on how to trade, the investor will lack direction. It may lead to spur-of-the-moment decisions, and the investor may regret these choices. There may be some periods where one will not trade, as it won't be as profitable. Perhaps the market is down, and the trader does not wish to sell any stock. Perhaps the market is up, and the trader does not want to buy any stock. There will be events such as vacations, holidays, stressful events, or emergencies. One must also consider how much money we have. Although it is possible to double one's money in a year, it is not likely for a beginner to do so. One may also choose to invest one time and hold it, or we may choose to invest more often into our account. This time and amount will depend on the investors and their financial situation.

The investor must also choose a strategy. They may wish to buy and sell stocks or to buy and hold stocks. They may even consider options trading. Whichever method that the investor chooses, there will be different goals to fit those strategies.

Long-term goals may be set to help the investor. Although planning for the following year may help the investor, longer periods may prove even more beneficial. Perhaps the investor wishes to acquire a million dollars' worth of stock in the next ten years. Perhaps the investor wishes to save a certain amount for retirement, which they wish to have in 25 years. Whatever the end goal is, the investor must make that clear so that they can begin working towards it immediately. Once a proper plan is created for meeting the investor's goals, they may move to the next step.

Choosing an Investment Method

After the investor has set goals and created a plan to meet them, it is time to decide on which investment method they wish to pursue. For those that wish to trade on their own completely, the DIY (do-it-yourself) method is the best fit. The investor may conduct all their trades online, making transfers from the bank manually or automatically. It will allow full control of one's investments. There will also be complete independence over what the investor wishes to buy and sell, how much, and how often they wish to trade. They will, however, need to dedicate time to researching on making any transfers, trading, and other procedures. There is also a higher risk for this choice, as a beginning investor will not have the education that a financial advisor will. Independent traders won't be under the control of a Robo-advisor. All the profit that is made by the investor will be theirs to keep; they won't have to pay commissions and fees, outside the one required by the broker that they use.

The least independent approach to investing in stock is by hiring a financial advisor. It is for those who do not wish to touch their stock at all and to have it fully regulated for them. Hesitant beginners may benefit from this method. It is important to remember, however, that this method tends to be expensive. It is most beneficial for those with higher assets and larger portfolios. It is also necessary to choose an investor that will work to meet the investor's goals, not just the goals of themselves. Therefore, the investor must set specific goals for themselves and how they wish to invest their money. They may more easily communicate to the advisor their goals, which must be satisfied.

Choosing a Stockbroker

When investing for oneself, a proper stockbroker must be chosen. This will depend on the individual's needs and wants. For some, their bank they already operate with offers stock investments. This is a quick and simple option, as their money will already be linked through the bank, and they may already be familiar with their style. The bank may also have some other options of financial advisors that are free-of-charge. Otherwise, the investor must research their options before settling on a broker.

When choosing a stockbroker, the investor should research any fees (transaction fees, maintenance fees, etc.), minimum funds required to open an account, any commission collected by the stockbroker, and accessibility. The investor may prefer a specific type of formatting for their broker to have. There may also be free education, customer service, and other ways to make investing easier for the investor.

The investor must choose the option that will allow them to make the highest return on their investments. The investor should keep in mind which services they are likely to use most frequently, and they should choose the broker that charges the least to use those services. There may be transactional fees, which are the costs of buying and selling stocks. Many beginning investors tend to forget this, so it is essential to take this into account.

Opening an Account

When opening an account, a few steps are often required. This is typically not a lengthy process, but the investor should be aware of the potential actions associated with this process. The first step when opening an online account is obviously to create an account. This will consist of a username and password, as well as some personal information, which may include setting goals, determining which types of features the investor wishes to use, and the investor's experience level. This information will help to create the optimal experience for the investor. There may also be an application for the account to ensure that the investor is qualified to hold the account. As well as an agreement stating that the investor assumes all the risks of investing and understands that the money is not insured or guaranteed.

Initial Investment and Linking Accounts.

During the application process, the investor will most likely be prompted to fund the account. This can be done in several ways. The investor may transfer the funds electronically via an EFT (Electronic funds transfer). This is transferring the money from a linked bank account and will most likely only take one business day to complete. The investor may also choose to make a wire transfer, which is a transfer directly from the bank. It is important to consider how much to invest in the account initially carefully. For those just starting, there may not be much money to invest at first. The minimum investment amounts for the broker should be considered over beforehand.

Buying and Selling Stocks

After the investor funds their account, it is time to start trading the stocks. It must be decided what stock, how much of the stock, and how the investor wishes to buy. Once these factors are decided, the investor must buy the stock. It is usually as simple as searching the stock symbol and selecting "buy." It is best to wait until the stock is at a low, but the investor must also begin investing as early as possible in experiencing the benefits. When the stock is bought, it will typically take a bit to process and for the broker to receive these funds. After that, it will appear in the investor's online portfolio. When it is time to sell this stock, the investor may typically visit their portfolio and click "sell" on the desired stock.

The best time to invest was 10 years ago. Another better time to invest is... Right Now!

Chapter 2.

Do's and Don'ts

Topic Covered:

- ◆ Do's

- ◆ Don'ts

You need to understand and realize a couple of things regarding stock investing. First, there is no sure-shot formula for profitable stock investing. Even the most successful and celebrated investors lose money in some cases. However, some rules are followed by many successful stock investors. These rules prove to be useful over a long period and enough stock trades. If you follow them prudently and consider the specifics of a stock or market condition, you may increase the chances of a good return on your investments.

Do's

- You should have a long-term approach to stock investing with a broad picture of your investment goals in your mind.

- It would be best if you had a thoroughly grounded and realistic perspective. Making money in stocks is not an easy task, and it takes time and effort to become successful at it. Persistence is vital when learning to invest. Don't get discouraged.

- As a new investor, be prepared to take some small losses. Experience is a great teacher.

- You'll need to do much research and develop a sound understanding of the stock market before getting to start.

- You should follow a well-disciplined investment approach. If you put in money systematically in the right stocks and hold on to your investments for enough period, you would increase your chances of generating good returns.

- It would help if you always made an informed decision. Do a proper analysis of the fundamentals of a stock before investing in that stock.

- It would help if you created a well-diversified portfolio by investing in several good stocks of well-known companies with leadership positions in their industries. Diversification will reduce your risks and heavy losses.

- You should invest in the right stocks or companies. Strong sales and earnings growth characterize these as well as increasing or good profit margins, consistent and high return on equity of 15% or more, industry leader or with large market share, etc.

- You should have realistic expectations. In times of bull runs, some stocks generated returns of 25% plus. However, you cannot take such a performance as your annual benchmark return for your stock investment. It may lead you to take unnecessary risks. You should aim for a return of 10%.

- You should monitor your stock investments or portfolio regularly and rigorously. This will help you in making desired changes in your portfolio with the evolving market conditions. Concentrate your eggs in a few solid baskets, know each of them well, and keep on watching them vigilantly.

- You should learn from great investors. It is advised to never invest in the stock, but to invest in the business. You should invest in a business or market that you understand. This will help you in judging the proper value of a company and its stock and consequently increase your chances of identifying good stocks for profitable investing.

- It is also important to pick the right broker with a good track record, online facilities, tools and apps, high-grade customer support, etc.

Don'ts

- In the beginning, do not invest in companies or sectors that are characterized by much volatility or fluctuations in stock prices.

- As a beginner, do not set up a margin account; but set up a cash account.

- You should avoid more volatile types of investments, at least in the initial phase, like futures, options, and foreign stocks.

- You should not buy a stock just because it is cheap. You generally get what you pay for.

- You should avoid the herd mentality and invest in a stock because your friends, relatives, or acquaintances are buying the stock. Always invest in a stock after you do your own research and once understand the fundamentals of that stock.

- You should not try to time the stock market. Catching the top or the bottom of the stock market is not a good idea. You may lose money in trying to time the market.

- Do not allow your emotions and sentiments to cloud your judgment regarding stock investments. Many investors have lost money, mainly due to their failure to control their emotions. These emotions are usually fear and greed.

- You should never speculate by building heavy positions in some stocks, buying stocks of unknown companies, etc. The fabulous dream to become a millionaire overnight may even wipe out your hard-earned money.

Chapter 3.

Technical Analysis Vs Fundamental Analysis

Topic Covered:

- Trend Seeking

- Support and Resistance

- Moving Averages

- Chart Patterns

- Bollinger Bands

- Value Investing and Growth Investing

- Fundamentals of Growth Investment Strategies

- Combination of Value and Growth Strategies

Technical analysis is a method of looking at stock charts and data to spot price trends. It is a method primarily used by traders who are interested in short term profits, but it can be helpful for long-term investors as well. Long-term investors can use technical analysis to determine (estimate) the best entry points into their positions. Note that technical analysis certainly isn't required, and most long-term investors ignore short-term trends and use dollar-cost averaging. Nonetheless, it's a good idea to become familiar with technical analysis in case you decide you want to use it in the future.

Fundamental analysis focuses on the underlying fundamentals of the company. These can include earnings, price to earnings ratio for the stock, and profit margins. The technical analysis ignores all these things and focuses on the trades of the moment. It seeks to discover upcoming trends in buying behavior. So, whether a company was profitable in the previous quarter—It doesn't necessarily matter. Of course, profitability can drive more stock purchases, and so drive up the price. But many things can drive the price up or down over the short term. Simple emotion can do it, and so traders that use technical analysis study the charts themselves and pay far less attention to external factors or fundamentals.

Trend Seeking

The first thing that technical analysis seeks to discover is the trend. Simply put, a trend is a prevailing price movement in one direction or the other. The period isn't specific and will depend on the trader's needs and goals. For example, day traders are looking for a trend that might only last two hours. Swing traders may hope to ride a trend that lasts weeks or months. Position traders are looking for longer-term changes and want to enter a position at a low price and exit that position month or between 1-2 years later at a higher price to make a profit.

Trends are easy to estimate, but your estimations have no guarantee of being correct. For an uptrend, traders typically draw straight lines through the low points of the gyrations of the stock on the graph. This will help you estimate where the trend will end up at some future point in time. You can use this to set a selling point when you exit your position.

Support and Resistance

Over relatively short periods, stocks will stay confined between a range of prices. The low pricing point of this range is called support. The upper price point of the range is called resistance. The trader seeks to enter their position at a point of support. They can also place a stop-loss order slightly below support so that they will exit the position if they bet wrong and share prices drop substantially. Then they can sell their stocks when the share price gets close to resistance levels, on the theory that it's more likely than not to drop back down after reaching resistance.

Moving Averages

The number of periods defines a moving average. So, if we were using a chart that is framed in terms of days, a 9-period moving average would be a 9-day moving average. This helps eliminate noise from the stock charts and can be useful in spotting trends.

The real benefit comes from comparing moving averages with different periods. A short period crosses above a long period moving average indicates that an upward trend in pricing can be expected. That's because it indicates that buyers are moving into the market more recently.

Conversely, when a short period crosses below a long period moving average, that indicates a coming downward trend in the market.

A simple moving average, one that simply calculates the average of the past given number of days, is going to give equal weight to prices days ago and prices more recently. This is an undesirable feature, and so traders prefer to use exponential moving averages to get more accurate data. Exponential moving averages weight the data, giving more importance to recent prices and less weight to more distant prices.

Chart Patterns

Traders also look for specific chart patterns that can indicate coming trend reversals. For example, you might be looking for signs that a stock is unable to move any higher in price after having undergone a large and long-lasting uptrend. What happens in these cases is that the stock price will touch or reach a certain price level that is slightly higher than where it is at present and do so two or more times. But each time it reaches the peak value, it will drop back down in price.

Traders also look for signals in the chart that a breakout is going to occur. A breakout can happen to the upside, that is, stock prices can increase a great deal, or it can happen to the downside, in which case a strong downward trend in share price will follow.

Bollinger Bands

Bollinger bands attempt to combine the idea of a moving average with moving zones of support and resistance. The levels of support and resistance for a stock are calculated at any given time using the standard deviation. Bollinger bands will include a simple moving average curve in the center to represent the mean stock price.

Value Investing and Growth Investing

Investing can further be divided into two main categories. These are value investing and growth investing. These two categories have been around for decades and have been used successfully by investors over the decades.

Value investing refers to the purchase of stocks of undervalued firms. The main purpose here is to identify the top companies with undervalued stock rather than investing in largely unknown firms whose potential is yet to be determined.

Most value investors prefer investing in stable and strong firms that appear not to reflect a company's real value. As such, they hope to benefit when the firm's real value is realized, and others show an interest in it.

You need to know what some of the pointers are. What are some of the factors that indicate a company's shares are undervalued? There are a couple of tips, including high dividend yield, but more important is a minimal price to book ratio. This is a ratio most preferred by value investors.

As it is, the marketplace is hardly accurate all the time. Sometimes there are errors and mistakes on how companies are valued. Some stocks are overvalued, while others are undervalued.

When these stocks are eventually valued correctly, they gain in value, and this gain will pass on to the investor. It can sometimes be a pretty significant gain, so this is the main reason why some investors go for value investing.

Sometimes this strategy can be a short-term affair but a long-term approach for other investors. While the strategy is rather straightforward and uncomplicated, it can be a little complicated, especially in the long term. Some investors hope to make a quick kill out of this strategy by making it short-term.

This can be a mistake because it may take a while before the real value of the firm is known. Therefore, if you wish to become a value investor, you should think about investing in the long term rather than short-term so that you receive real benefits. Also, most investors are into investing in the long term. As such, it is advisable to always think about long-term investing as well as long-term benefits which are much greater than quick, short, gains.

Fundamentals of Growth Investment Strategies

Growth investment is crucial when it comes to stock investing. It is one of the two pillars of stock investing, the other being value investing. There is a distinct difference between these two groups of investors.

One significant difference between these two investment models is that value investors approach is more focused on young companies with potential for above-average and significant growth in the coming years. On the other hand, growth investors focus on firms that have regularly displayed significant growth as well as a substantial increase in opportunities and profits.

There is an accepted theory behind the growth investment strategy. Investors think that an increase in revenue or earnings should result in increased share prices. Therefore, they prefer buying stocks that are priced either equal to or just above a company's latest intrinsic value.

This is often based on the belief that the inherent value of the firm will increase based on the continuous fast growth rate. There are specific metrics used by growth investors, and they include profit margin, EPS or earnings per share and ROE or return on equity.

Combination of Value and Growth Strategies

The best approach, according to finance experts, is to combine these two strategies, especially for investors seeking fast, long term growth. A combination of growth and value investing is known to be a successful one and is the approach adopted so successfully by the billionaire investor Warren Buffet. It is advisable to consider this approach because it promises an even more successful outcome, especially in the long term.

There are several reasons why this is a worthwhile pursuit. For starters, value stocks are mostly stocks of firms operating in cyclical industries.

Consumers spend their discretionary incomes in these industries only when they believe it is necessary.

Take, for instance, the airline industry. Consumers mostly choose to fly a lot when the economy is on an upward trajectory and then keep airlines when times are tough. As such, the airline industry is cyclical, and its stocks can be deemed to be value stocks.

As a result of seasonal gains and stagnation, value stocks tend to do well during times of prosperity and economic recovery, then perform rather dismally when a trending market is sustained for lengthy periods. Such stocks thrive during low-interest rate situations and grow even in the final stages of a long-running bull market. However, the minute that the economy experiences a downturn, these industries are the first to suffer loss.

If you choose, as an investor, both value and growth investing, you are likely to enjoy bigger returns even as you also reduce your risks substantially.

In theory, you will easily generate optimum profitability if you purchase stocks using both value and growth strategies.

And even though the economy fluctuates with each economic cycle, you will emerge the winner after things even out eventually.

Since you're already thinking, think big; Nothing and no one can stop you from doing so!

Chapter 4.

How to Build Your Investment Portfolio

Topic Covered:

- Building an Investment Portfolio

- Investing in Other Sectors

- Index Investing

- Investing in Real Properties

As an investor, you should not invest all your money in a single stock. This is very similar to putting all your eggs in one basket. Identify several stocks from different industries such as the financial services sector, industrial, automotive, oil and gas, transport, and so on. If you can identify some good shares in some of these sectors, then you will improve your chances of success at the stock markets. Statistics indicate that diversified portfolios are much more successful and earn more money that single stock portfolios. Diversification also saves you from imminent loss should anything negative happen. People have been known to lose their investments for a lack of diversification. For instance, let us assume you purchase Boeing stocks, and shortly after that, major incidents involving airplane crashes happen. The stock would plummet in value, and you would lose most of your investments.

When you invest in stocks, you need to be on the lookout for price changes regularly. Prices rise and fall based on a variety of factors. For instance, when interest rates fall, the economy will have a positive outlook, and stock prices will very likely rise. On the other hand, when an industry-specific incident happens, or the economy falls into recession, then prices are bound to fall. In general, the stock market is a static entity, and prices are always falling and rising. You should know when you want to benefit from this regular rise and all-in price, also known as volatility. You can benefit greatly by buying stocks when the price is low, then selling when prices go up. The main goal of any trader or investor is to take advantage of short-term price movements. We have learned that stocks are never static, and there is almost always some volatility in the markets. This volatility translated to price movements. A seasoned trader can monitor these movements and take advantage of them to profit in a big way. Most traders at the markets do this regularly. They spend their time monitoring the markets and observing price movement.

Take, for example, a person who has $10,000 they wish to invest in the stock market. You will first open an account with a broker then fund it with your trading capital. Once your account is up and running, you should scan the markets for the most suitable stocks. This will teach you how to identify such stocks. However, past performance at the markets and the company's fundamentals are examples of things to watch out.

Now, once you identify the desired stocks to buy, you should then purchase them in enough quantities. Remember to spread out your purchases and not to purchase just one stock. This way, you will spread out the risk and minimize exposure. As an investor, you will not engage in active trading even though you are free to do so.

Also, as an investor, you may not necessarily need a lump sum amount to invest in stocks. All that you will need is an amount as little as $100 plus fees and costs charged by your broker. However, it is advisable to grow your investments with time.

This means investing small amounts like $100 each week, or every fortnight or even monthly. This is how a lot of people in America grow their money. They invest in the stock market and then grow their investments over time. The income generated is then used for other purposes such as capital to start a business or a down payment for a home.

Building an Investment Portfolio

As an investor, the best approach is diversification. Diversification means investing your funds in different securities. This is highly advisable because of the inherent and underlying risks posed by the markets. It is a fact that the price or value of stocks keeps changing almost all the time. Diversification means no matter what happens, you can still be profitable.

Therefore, to invest wisely, you will need to develop or come up with a suitable investment portfolio. It is easy to imagine an investment portfolio where all your investments are held.

A portfolio is in other ways like a safe that stores crucial personal or business documents. However, unlike a safe, it is more of a concept rather than a tangible product.

When you diversify your investments into a portfolio, it means that you will own a myriad of assets. These assets could be exchange-traded funds or ETFs, mutual funds, bonds, stocks, and many others. However, it is best to approach the diversification of a portfolio with a well-thought-out plan and not haphazardly.

We can define portfolio management as an approach to balancing rewards and risks. To meet your investment goals, you will need to invest in a wide variety of products, including SMAs, REITs, closed-end funds, ETFs and others. It is an excellent idea and highly recommended to have an investment plan and determine what your end goal is, especially when there are numerous options available.

Portfolio management often means different things to different investors. Think about a young person fresh from college and on his first job. Such a person views portfolio management as a way of growing investments and providing a pretty decent amount over time for future use.

Such a person will view portfolio management as an excellent chance of holding on to their wealth, possibly accumulated over the years. There are different ways of organizing and planning portfolio management.

A portfolio manager should be able to handle the various needs that different investors have when coming up with a diversified portfolio.

Therefore, the individualized approach is a highly advised option. Here are some basic principles for developing a portfolio.

It is advisable to note the availability of numerous options. A client or investor needs to determine whether they wish to create wealth over time, put away funds for future use, generate a regular income, and so on. This way, it will be possible to come up with a suitable investment plan. Such a plan should incorporate appetite for risk, period, and similar aspects.

By spreading your wealth into different types of investment vehicles, you prevent one type of risk from wiping out the entire value of your portfolio. Here are some strategies that you can use to diversify your asset distribution:

- **Investing in Other Sectors**

If your portfolio value is still small, you may consider diversifying by investing in the other sectors. Make sure that you learn about the new sector first, and the companies in it before you pull the trigger. Investing in a second sector widens your circle of competence. It increases the number of companies that you can invest in safely. It also allows you to spread your funds to another industry so that you will be able to avoid exposing your money to one type of sector-related risk. One way to do this is by dividing your portfolio fund into two. You could leave one of the funds you first invested in. You could then distribute the other half in the new sector you've selected. You could also go about it by leaving your old positions alone and investing only new funds into the new sector. This strategy is better if you are in no position to sell your older positions. With this strategy, you will be building up your fund in the new sector from scratch.

• Index Investing

Index investing is another strategy that you can use to diversify your fund's distribution. With this method of investing, you no longer need to spend too much time doing fundamental analysis. Instead, you only spread your wealth among the companies in the index you have chosen. This method of investing is used by people who believe that it is impossible to beat the market consistently. This belief has some statistical backing. In the year 2010, more than 90% of fund managers failed to beat the performance of the S&P 500. Most of the managers who did beat the market were significant in hedge funds, mutual funds and banks that were only accessible to the rich. Because you are a beginner, we could assume that you will not be able to beat the performance of the market in your first year of trading. If you believe this too, you may be better of using the index investing method. To invest in an index fund, you will need to pick a company to do it. You could then ask them if they are offering index funds. The best time to start investing in an index fund is when the market is doing well. Index funds tend to be of higher risk compared to other types of mutual funds. They are riskier than other types of managed funds like balanced funds and equity funds because of the tendency of its price to fluctuate. However, this higher risk is directly proportional to the potential rewards that you may get.

• Investing in Other Types of Securities

If your goal is to maximize your diversification, you could also consider investing outside of the stock market. If your funds are totally invested in the stock market, you are exposing 100% of it to stock market-related risks. As your funds grow bigger, you may want to put some of it in other types of securities. One option that you may consider bonds. While company stocks are regarded as equity investments, bonds are considered debt investments. The companies and government agencies who issue these bonds are basically borrowing money from you. The bond is the proof of the transaction, and it states the amount of money borrowed, the schedule of repayment and the interest rate of the loan.

Aside from bonds, you may also choose to invest in commodities. Commodities trading applies a similar trading strategy as stocks, in that it requires you to buy low and sell high.

- **Investing in Real Properties**

If your fund grows in value, you may also invest in properties. Investing in another type of asset, one that is tangible, can increase the diversity of your asset distribution. Investing in real estate, though, just like any type of investment, requires you to study what you are buying. You also need to time your entry into the market.

If the price of real estate in your area is low compared to its potential value, you may choose to use it as your method of diversifying your income.

There are multiple ways that you can earn through real estate investing. Just like with securities, you can also buy and sell properties. You also have the option of renting your properties out.

Chapter 5.

Master the Stocks Market

Topic Covered:

- Investment Club
- Two Kinds of Markets and How to Trade Them
- The Price to Earnings (P/E) Indicator
- Earnings Growth and Quality
- Average Day by Day Volume
- Stock Volatility

There are numerous ways of investing in stocks. All these ways have some advantages and disadvantages, but every individual's situation is different. What's right for you may lead to a problematic situation for another. Considering the period and market value, while looking for stocks to invest in, is highly recommended.

Sometimes, the market may be going through a smooth and steady path, and your emotional aspects may get in the way to make the right decision.

You may invest in expensive stocks due to the success of the market. On the other hand, in a poorly performing market during situations like inflation, you may start to sell off your stocks.

So how can you decide where to invest? First off, you need to analyze how much a specific investment method would be affected by the risk and potential losses. If the risk is too high, but the gains from it would be more fruitful, you would know what step to take. Such decision making requires proper research of all the methods, and a proper understanding of how much would be at stake, in different situations.

We know that all methods would have specific effects, but in the end, the success relies on how much risk you are ready to take, as well as how much knowledge you have in stock marketing. If you're into a more modern and technological way of business, then you should know, online buying of stocks is a thing.

However, it is only recommended if you know how the stock market operates and can give useful advice to yourself, as this one doesn't involve any advice to be given, so you're on your own. Also, it is far riskier, as you are charged only a flat fee for each transaction. Also, to mention, it's time-consuming, as you would have to train yourself until you're confident enough to take the next step.

Investment Club

The next method which you can consider is through the investment clubs. You meet a lot of people who may be going through the same situation you are, and people who can give professional and financial advice. Other people's experiences can make you learn a lot too. It is affordable and can help you to understand and differentiate between different market situations. Increased involvement and investing in stocks through this can help you gain a new perspective and a sense of direction.

If you purchase some clothes and neglect the fact that trying them on would help you decide whether to buy them or not and come home to only find out that the clothes don't fit, you'll be pretty disappointed unless there is an exchange or return policy at the outlet. If not, you're at a loss. Trust me, investing in a market is nothing close to purchasing clothes. Hence, neglecting important facts can lead to the loss of a fortune. Investing in stock markets is nothing close to managing your day-to-day spending. So, you got to be smart about it.

Investing in stocks for the first time has a much higher risk. However, these risks are to be taken, but as mentioned before, there is always supposed to be a margin. The potential risk still needs to be managed.

Research gets you a long way. You don't want to trust the company blindly. It is important to analyze and study how the company is doing in the market. Their marketing tactics, financial weaknesses, and productivity need to be kept in mind.

If the business doesn't have a good marketing department, it's likely to go crashing down as soon as the competition gets tough. The finance department needs to be checked and observed at every point, as they handle a major part of the business. Any fishy business being done, the greater is the effect on you. Whatever the company is selling, it needs to have a good production plan, method, and a skilled and efficient workforce.

Two Kinds of Markets and How to Trade Them

Several markets facilitate trade in exchange for assets. Each market runs under different trading mechanisms, which seem to affect liquidity and control of the company. A positive effect on the liquidity of the market would mean the ball being in your court.

The Dealers Market

The dealer's market is the type of market in which the dealer acts as a counterparty between the seller and the buyer. He sets the bid and asks the prices for the security in question. Any investor, who accepts the price, would be involved in the trade.

The term 'over the counter' dealers emerged from this when dealers sell securities. This leads to increased liquidity in the market, which means a lesser risk of bankruptcy and loss. The market would be able to get out of its debt without selling the assets. This would happen at the cost of a small premium. In this, you would expect an additional return, for holding a risky market portfolio, instead of risk-free assets.

In this market, the dealer holds counterparty risk. He often sets the bid prices lower than the market price and asks for higher premium instead. In this way, the spread between the prices will be the profit the dealer would make.

Such markets are more common in bonds and currencies, instead of stocks. There are more future opportunities for many dealers in this market. It holds more long-term future success and options, as well as useful for derivatives. One important aspect of this is that foreign exchange markets are usually dealt with within the dealer's market. The banks and currency exchange acts as the dealer intermediary. The dealer market is known as the most liquid market. Hence, it is good for you, as a beginner, as paying the debts would be easier.

The Exchange Market

The exchange market is one is known to be the most automated, but the irony is that, without the presence of a buyer and the seller, there is no execution of the trade.

In this market, no brokers are used for stock trading, as the order matches the buyers and the sellers. This is a quicker and less time-consuming method, which also avoids any delay in the trade to take place. However, the buyers and sellers are expected to find a counterparty, as there is no involvement of a broker or a dealer intermediary.

Exchanges are most appropriate for standardized securities, including stocks, bonds, futures, contracts, and options. Exchanges will typically specify characteristics for the securities traded on the exchange.

Fundamental Analysis

Those who trade based only upon the return offered and who do not evaluate the fundamentals are not in the game very long. Fundamental analysis is more detailed than the elements presented here. The goal is to assure we of the stock's worthiness and to look for danger signs. If a stock does not cut, you should find it quickly to waste as little time as possible. For this reason, the most important fundamental elements are viewed first.

The Price to Earnings (P/E) Indicator

The P/E ratio is not perfect and reveals to us nothing about the nature of profit, or whether income is growing or taking a downturn. Be that as it may, it regardless fills in as a valuable measurement to look at stocks in a similar industry. A P/E ratio is fundamentally higher than the business average outcomes because the market prefers the stock, yet that preference can change abruptly. If market opinion changes negatively towards that stock, you, as a holder of that stock can sell it. Sell off would be more worthwhile if the stock sold for an overvalued price.

Earnings Growth and Quality

On numerous occasions, earnings, including one-time, unprecedented events, are unimportant to earnings quality. By quality, we allude to operational profit (and income), not phenomenal occasions like the offer of a division or a one-time discount. What's more, companies that focus more on earnings, usually report their financial outputs to show more earning quality. Now and then, these incomes exhibited here are sometimes misdirecting. Tragically, profit quality is hard to evaluate without a point-by-point assessment of the companies' financial statements. Hence, you may wish to concentrate on earnings development over time and its dependability, since robust earnings growth is a more applicable metric than earning quality. Earnings per share (EPS) is emphasized in this respect since it relies upon the number of offers exceptional. A stock buyback would blow up EPS without a relating income increment. What's more, giving new offers such as public offerings, mergers, etc. would diminish EPS, yet the money inflow may be very positive.

Average Day by Day Volume

Although this is more a technical analysis tool, it is also very relevant in this discussion. Volume is, by and large, a proportion of the stock's liquidity and dependability, however not really of its necessary sufficiency. Low-volume stocks can give high returns; however, they are dependent upon control and cannot move much of a stretch. There are an excessive number of incredible assets with substantial volume to allow for the trading of the low-volume stocks. Regardless of whether you are searching for progressively unstable stocks for exchanging openings, pick high volume. The average day by day volume is what makes a difference.

Stock Volatility

Volatility reveals to us how unpredictable the stock is, take the most recent incident; for example, Tesla, how has been it rose and dropped sharply in the market. Instability might be level when contrasted with records, and it can also be expanding or diminishing. Then there is implied volatility that demonstrates whether alternative prices are inferring a potential future unpredictability that is lower than or higher than the records of volatility.

Remember that the markets frequently show general volatility of under 15%. 20-40% is a medium degree of instability, and over 40% could be viewed as high. Over 80% is high as can be. Choose what instability level you are eager to go up against. However, staying with more prominent companies with reliable records in the twenty to fifty percent volatility range, can yield enormous profits for your investment. Inferred or implied volatility should be estimated against the 10-day volatility. If implied volatility is following the lower 30-day unpredictability rather than the higher 10-day instability, at that point, the later volatility primarily isn't being estimated into the choice; the market isn't worried about it because there is no cause for alarm. A final group you should consider are the Insiders (officials, chiefs, and significant investors). They are bound to record reports when they purchase or sell protections of their companies. These reports are broadly held to demonstrate whether the insiders think about their organization's stock a purchase or a short. This view is commenced on chronicled perceptions that insiders will, in general, purchase their organization's stock when the viewpoint is splendid and sell in front of terrible occasions for the organization. This means well since they have a definitive instructive favorable position.

Many analyses and forces affect when to choose stocks, how to choose them, when to sell, and hold on to your stock. A strong understanding of these factors and their respective fluctuations would help make you an investment guru.

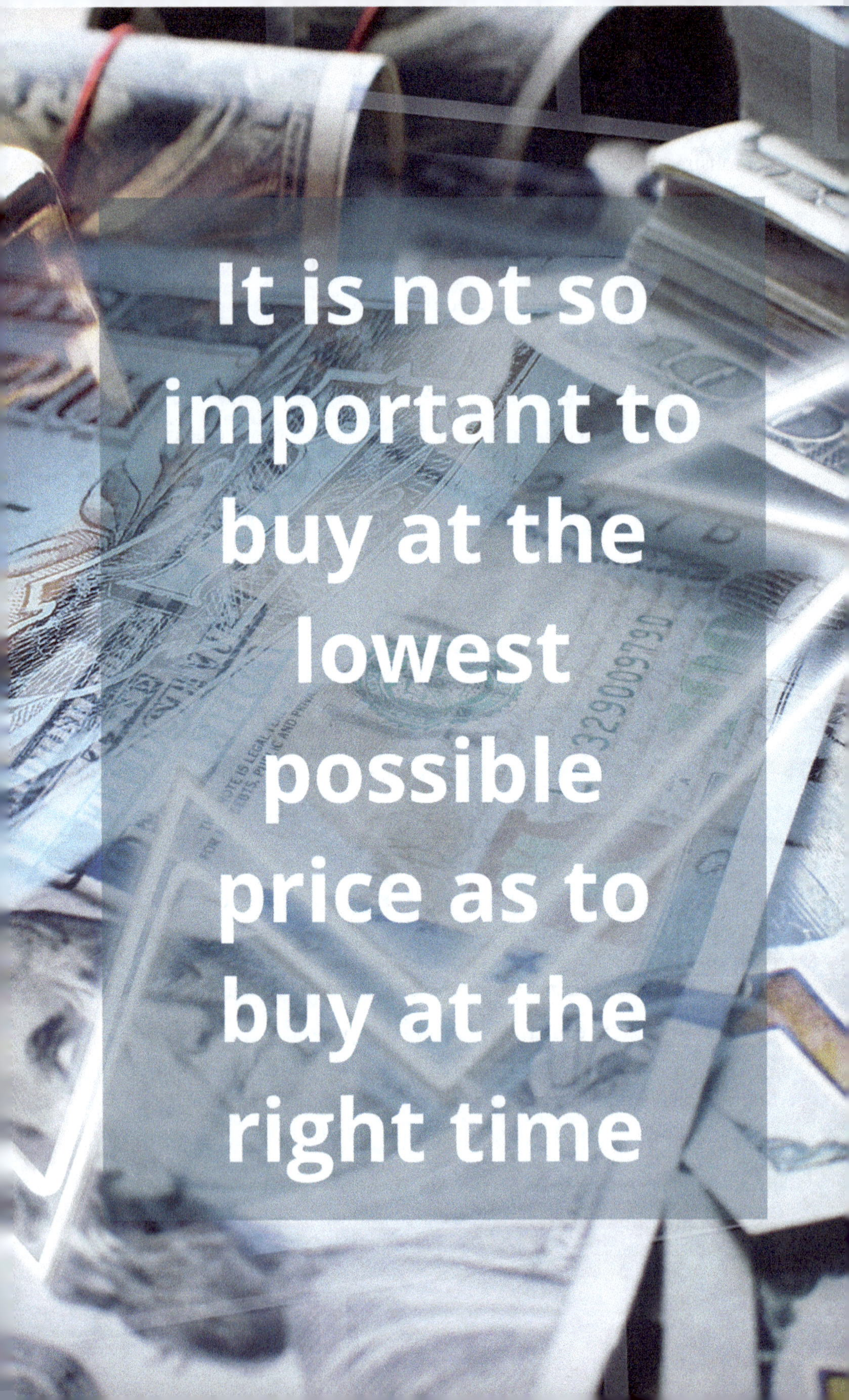
It is not so important to buy at the lowest possible price as to buy at the right time

Chapter 6.

Dividend Stocks Creating Passive Income

Topic Covered:

- Benefits of Dividend Investing

- How to Pick Dividends

- Size of Payout

For hundreds of years, long-term investors participated in dividend stocks. At the beginning of the 20th century, most of the money made in the stock market in the US came in the form of dividends that companies paid to their shareholders. It is one of the opportunities that an average investor can enjoy now, too. This age is dominated by speculation in various securities. People tend to believe that they can make a killing in the stock market by selecting the right stock that would rise by a thousand percent and win a jackpot. Unfortunately, most speculators end up losing it all.

They ignore long-term profits and tend to choose short-term strategies to invest in stocks. Very few investors now think about a company in terms of whether it pays dividends or not. Most are searching for growth stocks that start their existence in the market from $5 or something and, in a matter of a few years, skyrocket to $100 or even more. They search for future stocks of CISCO, Wal-Mart, Apple, or Google that are going to fly like rockets to the moon and make them wealthy beyond their wildest dreams. Very few find these stocks. Some pick up some penny stocks and lose a substantial amount of their money investing in them.

However, the facts speak for themselves. Some say that for the past 100 years or so, more than forty percent of the famous S&P500 returns came from dividends. The statistics should make one think whether it is better to leave short-term strategies and concentrate on the long-term ones. One of the best strategies is, of course, investing in dividend stocks. When you start delving into the subject, you will see how many advantages this kind of investing has over other most popular trading strategies. Let us look through some of the benefits of buying and holding dividend-paying stocks.

Benefits of Dividend Investing

You earn from dividends and rising share prices. So, this shows that there is a possibility to make money in two ways. Firstly, you get dividends, and most are paid quarterly. Secondly, you can also make substantial amounts of money from a rise in your shares. As you know, stocks rise and fall, and since you are in these dividend stocks for the long haul, you will surely benefit in these two ways: from steady dividends and rising prices of your stocks.

- **Steady income year after year**

Those who only expect to make money as shares rise will often have to sit out through bear markets when all stocks are falling, and they do not get the privilege of getting a steady income from the market in those times. However, those who own dividend stocks can enjoy never-ending streams of cash in good times and bad. Even if your shares' price is falling, your dividends are still paid, and your steady stream of income never stops.

- **The power of compounding when reinvesting your dividends**

Some investors talk about the power of compounding that they get when they reinvest the dividends. In a nutshell, compounding is getting current/future earning from previous earnings. So, if you get dividends and use them to buy more shares of a company that pays them, next time, you will get more dividends (and consequently more cash). If you invest those, you will again get more shares and more dividends. These earning will keep growing if you continue doing this, year after year until you retire and have probably created yourself a nest egg.

This type of investment protects your wealth from losing its value during inflation. We do know that during inflation, money starts losing its value. As prices grow, your money gets less and less power to buy things due to rising prices. For centuries, investors have tried to protect their hard-earned cash gold and in dividend stocks. Inflation often follows an overheated economy when everything is booming, and various new businesses spring up. That's when companies make bigger profits and, consequently, pay more significant dividends. Your price of shares rises, and so do the dividends from depreciation by investing in

- **Dividend stocks outperform those that do not pay dividends**

Growth stocks may do very well during booms. However, as fast as they rise, they plummet when financial bubbles burst. Those who have held to those stocks lose all their profits and even more. Dividend stocks may not take you for such an extraordinary ride upward, but they will also not take you down hard when the economy heads south. So, those who follow long-term investment strategies and do not jump in and out of the market try to get a quick buck and will earn cash in good times and bad. Value stocks that they hold make them money even during very bad times because dividends do not stop coming. On the other hand, those who have been following short-term strategies have no streams of income from the market in bad times, and they need to wait for another boom to make money from rising prices in stocks. These stocks provide you with financial safety and stability. As people grow older, they want less risk and more stability and security. That is what investing in dividend stocks is all about. You protect yourself from falling markets by keeping a steady stream of income. Prices of these stocks are often cheaper, but as dividends rise with prices of shares, you earn more. In the same fashion as gold, dividend stocks have proven to be one of the safest ways to invest in the stock market. It relieves you from the pressure of where to enter and exit the market. Short-term investors are very concerned as to where they must enter and exit the market. They intend to capitalize on fast stock price moves, and it is crucial to be right when the move starts. Long-term dividend investors do not have to worry about that. They select the best-paying dividend stocks and accumulate their wealth slowly but surely. They do not have psychological pressure regarding daily market fluctuations, as they know they are there for the long haul.

How to Pick Dividends

There is no magic key to tell you exactly how to pick the winning dividend. That magic key would be almost as good as a lottery tracker that would tell you the exact number to choose. Make sure you are picking everything in the right way so that when the time comes, you can truly cash in on the dividends. Choosing the right ones will allow you to do so more quickly and give you the chance to make even more money.

Profits in the Company

The company profits are the number one thing that you should look at when you decide whether to choose them for your dividend investment. A company needs to have high profits for you to choose them, and they need to show that they are going to have these profits for a long time in the future. Ensure that the profits are going in the right direction and to make sure that you are going to be able to make money from the investment that you make. A company that has good profits is good.

Size of Payouts

You can always check the size of the payouts that the company has made to find out possible payments you can expect from the company. By simply looking at the company's trading profile, you will be able to see how much they payout, how often, and what it takes out of the profits that they have made. When you look at this amount, you need to consider all the aspects of the payouts, and this also includes the initial investment amount. Compare that amount to what you are planning on investing in the company and see if the payouts will be worth what you are going to invest in the company.

It is vital to ensure that you are looking at all this information in a way as if you were going to invest in the company.

Just because a company has great profits and appears to be healthy does not mean that it will continue to be healthy. One of the most popular cases to look at is the case of Whole Foods Market. They are a huge company that has a lot of help from the people who shop and the profits they make. They did well when the crunchy organic movement was happening, but their health has failed drastically since the recession hit. They are no longer profiting in the way that they would have been. When you are considering an investment, consider the future health of the company.

If you are hoping to make money from these companies, you can always invest more money into it so that you can get higher payments.

Be sure that you choose a company that works with you because that is what you want. Do not decide to invest your money in a company because a book or someone else told you. Do your own research, learn about the companies, and figure out exactly what you want to get out of the investment opportunity.

Chapter 7.

Make Money with Growth Stocks

Topic Covered:

- Ignore the High P/E

- Understanding IPO's

- Greatest IPOs

- Lenders and the IPO Process

A growth stock is simply the stock of any company that is expected to grow its revenues or earnings rapidly. Here's the first rule for trading growth stocks:

Ignore the High P/E

Great companies that are rapidly growing will always trade at high P/E's. They might not even have any earnings. They might be losing a lot of money as they grow their market share, like Uber. They might also grow their market share for many years before they turn on the profit spigot.

That's what Facebook did. It raised the social network for many years, before finally turning on advertising.

Value investors will always tell you to stay away from companies with high P/E's or companies that are losing money. But if you do that, you will miss some of the greatest stock runs of all time. Microsoft, Starbucks, Home Depot, and Amazon all traded at very high P/Es for many years. Amazon still does. But these stocks have gone on to make their holders very rich.

Companies with high P/E's are pricing in high growth in future earnings. If the growth is slowing or that those earnings may never appear, the market will trash the stock. That's why we always trade growth stocks with a clear stop loss.

If you are Warren Buffett investing in a mature company, the P/E does matter. If you are holding a growth stock for a few weeks or even months, nothing could matter less than the P/E.

Let me explain how to trade growth stocks:

I like to buy growth stocks that are hitting new 52-week highs, or even all-time new highs. This may seem counter-intuitive to some. Isn't it risky to purchase a stock that is at all-time new highs? Doesn't that mean that it has further to fall?

If you study the highest growth stocks of the past, you will notice that they spend a lot of time trading at all-time new highs. This makes sense simply because any stock that goes up a lot must spend a lot of time trading at new highs.

There is, in fact, something wonderful and magical about a stock at an all-time high: Every single holder of the stock has a profit.

By contrast, when a stock has crashed or is continuously hitting new 52-week lows, many investors and traders have been left holding the bag. If the stock then tries to rally, these investors will be happy to get out by selling their shares at their break-even price. This provides constant downward pressure, and thus makes it more difficult for the stock to bounce back.

At a new all-time high, everyone who owns the stock has a profit. All the losers are gone and have already exited at a loss or their break-even price. At new highs, there are only happy traders and investors left. Well, except for one group of traders that no one feels sympathy very much for the short-sellers. These are traders who have shorted the stock (probably because "it has such a high P/E") and are betting that it will go down. At a new all-time high, everyone who has shorted the stock previously now has a losing trade on their hands. They are sweating bullets.

And there's only one thing that they can do to stem their losses: They must "cover" their shorts by buying back the stock. This buying only adds more fuel to the fire, driving the stock higher, and forcing out more short sellers.

Meanwhile, a stock that has recently moved up a lot begins to be featured on CNBC and explained by online commentators. This publicity brings in a new wave of buyers, who continue to drive the stock higher and make it hit even more new all-time highs.

The next step is to look at a daily chart of each stock. I want to make sure that the stock is trading above its 50-day moving average; and that the 50-day moving average is above the 200-day moving average.

Never buy a growth stock if the stock is trading below its 200-day moving average, or if the 50-day moving average is trading below the 200-day moving average. If either of those two criteria is true, the stock is in a downtrend. There is nothing more dangerous than a growth stock in a downtrend. A growth stock might go up 300% over three years, and then fall 80-95% once it enters a downtrend. This can happen even with major companies.

If a growth stock is trading above its 50-day moving average, and the 50-day moving average is trading above the 200-day moving average, I am happy to belong. If the stock is trading at new 52-week highs or all-time highs, that's even better. If a stock gaps up to new highs after a strong earnings report, that can be a great buy signal. Due to an anomaly called "Post-Earnings-Announcement Drift" (PEAD), a stock that has gapped up like this will tend to continue moving in the same direction for many days or even weeks. As a small investor, you can ride the wave, as larger institutional investors add to their positions over time, causing the stock to drift higher.

Understanding IPO's

IPO (Initial Public Offering) is viewed as a privately-owned business that has developed with a moderately modest number of investors, including early speculators like the originators, family, and companions alongside expert financial specialists, such as financial speculators or holy messenger speculators.

IPO furnishes the organization in collecting a great deal of cash and gives a more prominent capacity to develop and grow. The expanded straightforwardness and offer posting validity can likewise be a factor in helping it acquire better terms when looking for obtained assets.

The first sale of Bear parts of an association is esteemed through due underwriting steadiness. When an association opens to the world, the once private offer ownership changes over to open ownership, and the present private financial specialists' offers become worth the open exchanging cost. Generally, the private to open advancement is a key time for private examiners to exchange out and win the benefits they were envisioning. Private speculators may grasp their ideas in the open market or sell a piece or all of them for augmentations.

Meanwhile, the open market opens an enormous open entryway for some money related authorities to buy shares in the association and contribute subsidizing to an association's financial specialists' worth. The open involves any individual or institutional monetary master who is enthusiastic about placing assets into the association.

As a rule, the number of offers the association sells and the expense for which offers sell are the making factors for the association's new financial specialists' worth. Financial specialists' worth is still controlled by examiners when it is both private and open. Anyway with an IPO the speculators' worth augmentation will be on a very basic level with cash from the fundamental issuance.

Greatest IPOs

- Alibaba Group (BABA) in 2014 raising $25 billion

- American Insurance Group (AIG) in 2006 raising $20.5 billion

- VISA (V) in 2008 raising $19.7 billion

- General Motors (GM) in 2010 raising $18.15 billion

- Facebook (FB) in 2012 raising $16.01 billion

Lenders and the IPO Process

An IPO involves two areas. One, the pre-advancing time of the promotion. Two, the primary clearance of Bear itself. Exactly when an association is excited about an IPO, it will elevate to underwriters by mentioning private offers, or it can, in like manner, possess an open articulation to make interest.

The underwriters lead the IPO technique and are picked by the association. An association may pick one or a couple of agents to supervise different bits of the IPO technique agreeably. The lenders are related to each piece of the IPO due to constancy, document course of action, recording, publicizing, and issuance.

Steps to an IPO going with:

1. Underwriters present suggestions and valuations discussing their organizations, the best sort of security to issue, offering esteem, the proportion of offers, and assessed time apportioning for the market promoting.

2. The association picks its underwriters, and authoritatively agrees to ensure terms through an embracing understanding.

3. IPO gatherings are confined, including agents, legitimate counsels, guaranteed open clerks, and Securities and Trade Commission masters.

4. Information as for the association is amassed for required IPO documentation.

- The S-1 Registration Statement is the basic IPO recording report. It has two areas: The arrangement and subtly held account information. The S-1 joins basic information about the ordinary date of the account. It will be adjusted as often as possible, all through the pre-IPO process. The included blueprint is in a similar manner refreshed interminably.

5. Marketing materials are made for pre-publicizing of the new Bear issuance.

- Underwriters and authorities promote the offer issuance to measure solicitation and set up a last offering expense. Underwriters can revise their money related examination all through the advancing technique. This can consolidate changing the IPO cost or issuance date as they see fit.

- Associations figure out how to meet unequivocal open offer on essentials. Associations must hold quick to both exchanges, posting essentials and SEC necessities for open associations.

A common hold is a kind of money related vehicle made up of a pool of funds assembled from various examiners to place assets into insurances, for instance, Bears, protections, cash market instruments, and multiple assets. Normal resources are worked by master money directors, who allocate the savings in favorable circumstances and attempt to convey capital increments or pay for the store's specialists. A typical store's portfolio is sorted out and kept up to match the endeavor targets communicated in its framework.

Regular backings give close to nothing, or individual specialist access to expertly supervised courses of action of esteems, bonds, and various securities. Each financial specialist, along these lines, takes an action, generally in the increments or hardships of the store. Normal resources put assets into many assurances, and execution is pursued as the modification in the outright market top of the save.

In this business, if you are good, you are right six times out of ten. You're never right nine times out of ten.

Chapter 8.

Investment Strategies

Topic Covered:

- Buy Depressed Assets
- Dollar-Cost Averaging
- Buy Self Liquidating Assets
- Smart Money Valuation

Now that you have an idea of why you need to invest and some fundamental principles in investment, as well as asset classes, you must feel ready to invest. For you to start winning in a big way, you will need the time; you must put a lot of effort; you should have the proper experience and groundwork to make that happen. And in many cases, even with the best-laid plans and with the best strategies laid out, things still don't pan out. The recommendation is simple: do the best with the situation you are facing. In other words, use specific strategies that would enable you to position yourself to come out ahead. They might not necessarily result in you making tons of money or experiencing truly stupendous returns, but they can position you for solid gains. The following strategies enable you to do just that.

Buy Depressed Assets

Now, this might seem straightforward. After all, this is just a reiteration of the classic investment and commercial maxim of "buy low, sell high." However, the big challenge here is in determining what constitutes a "depressed asset."

You might be thinking that a stock that was trading at $50 and pops to $150 might not be all that depressed if it fell to $100. You might be thinking, where's the depression? This is not a fire sale. It hasn't fallen enough.

If you look at the stock's trajectory and how much growth potential and market attention, it might very well turn out that the stock is headed to $300. Do you see how this works?

If that's the case, then scooping up the stock at the price of $100 after it fell from $150 is a steal. After all, buying something worth $300 for a third of its price is one heck of a bargain.

Now, the big issue here is how do you know the stock's full future value? This is where serious analysis comes in. You can't just buy stocks on hype. It would be best if you looked at facts that would inform the growth trajectory of that stock.

For example, is it a market leader? Does it have certain drugs in the approval pipeline that have little to no competition? Is it on the cusp of a breakthrough drug patent? Is it in the process of buying out its competition?

There are many factors that you should consider, which can impact the overall future value of a stock. You should pay attention to its current developments, and you should pay attention to the news cycle surrounding the company. You should also pay attention to its industry. Is its industry fast-expanding, or is it a "sunset industry" on its last legs? If it's in a sunset industry, there might still be opportunities there because usually, such industries witness a tremendous amount of consolidation. Whatever the case may be, always be on the lookout for the future value of a stock based on what you know now, as well as its past performance.

Dollar-Cost Averaging

What happens if you buy a stock that subsequently crashes? This happens to the very best of us. If this happened to you, don't get depressed. Don't think that you suck at investing. Don't think that all is lost. If you get caught in a downturn, it might be an amazing opportunity. Now, it's important to note that almost all stocks experience a pullback. I have yet to come across a stock that has appreciated positively with no dips in its trading history. I'm not aware of a stock that hasn't experienced a day-to-day dip in pricing. All stocks experience a pullback. Even stocks that are well on their way to becoming breakthrough or high-valued stocks will experience dips. What happens if you bought a stock that drops in value tremendously? Well, you have two options at this point. You can wait for the stock to keep going up and then start buying some more. You're taking bets on its recovery.

The better approach would be to use this as an opportunity. For example, if you bought, for the sake of simplicity, one share of stock at $100 a share, and the price crashes 50% to $50 a share, you can buy one share at $50, and this would average out your holdings to $75 per share. Ideally, you should wait for the stock to drop so much and then buy a whole lot. This enables you to set your break-even point at a much lower level. For example, using the same hypothetical facts mentioned above, instead of buying one share, you buy 9 shares at $50. So, what happens is, the average price per share gets reduced to $55. Even if the depressed stock manages to limp along and possibly pop up here and there, it doesn't have to pop up all that much to get all your money back from your position because once it hits $55, you're at break-even territory. Compare this with breaking even at $75 or, worse yet, waiting for the stock to come back to $100 a share. It's anybody's guess whether it will back to that level. This strategy is called dollar-cost averaging, and it is very useful. You must have free cash available, and you must use that free cash at the right time. That's how you maximize its value. That's how you fully take advantage of opportunities that present themselves. Otherwise, you might be in a situation where the stock crashes so hard that you could have broken even very easily with little money spent, but unfortunately, you were locked out because you don't have the cash to do it.

Buy Self Liquidating Assets

Another investing strategy you can take is to buy assets that pay for themselves. For example, if you spent a million dollars buying a building, but the building generates rents totaling $100,000 per year, the building pays for itself in roughly 13 years or more, factoring taxes and other costs.

Self-liquidating assets may seem too good to be true, but they are very real. Most of this applies to certain types of real estate, like commercial properties. However, this strategy also applies to stocks and bonds. For example, if you buy stocks that have no dividend and you buy bonds, you can use the bond interest to start paying off your stock's portfolio. Of course, this can take quite a bit of time if you factor in interest rates as well as taxes.

Smart Money Valuation

Another winning strategy is to buy into private corporations as a sophisticated investor at a much lower valuation. Now keep in mind that many mobile app companies are popping up all over the United States. You don't necessarily have to live in Silicon Valley of California to have access to these types of companies. The great thing about these companies is that in the beginning, they require very little capital. Many require "Angel," "per-Angel," or even raw seed capital. The founder would have a rough idea of a software, an app, or a website. This is the most basic stage of a company's evolution. Now, when you come in as a source of seed capital, you can lock into a large chunk of the company's stock for a very low valuation. For example, somebody comes up with a startup idea, and the initial cost is a maximum of $1 million. If you were to invest $250,000, you have a 25% stake in the company. You may be thinking that 25% of a company that's not worth that much, which is very, very risky, doesn't seem like a winning proposition. Well, keep in mind that after the seed stage, the company's valuation usually goes up. So, once your money has been used to push the company further along its developmental path, the company's valuation starts to go up, especially if they now have something more concrete to show other investors. You may be asking yourself, okay, the smart money valuation thing sounds awesome.

This is great in theory, but is it real? How can the Average Joe investor get in on such deals? There are websites like Angel List and others, as well as LinkedIn groups that publicize startup projects that are actively recruiting investors. Of course, you need to do your homework and pay attention to the track record of the founders.

Chapter 9.

Common Mistakes to Avoid

Topic Covered:

- Failure to Understand the Trade

- Impatience

- Failure to Diversify

- Getting Too Connected with a Certain Company

- Investment Turnover

- Timing the Market

- Trading with Emotions

- Setting Unrealistic Expectations

- Using Borrowed Money

Mistakes happen in every field, sector, and industry. Some are always anticipated, while others happened unexpectedly. When it comes to stock trading, there are several mistakes that you can make. Understanding these mistakes can help you avoid them, thus ending up successful in your stock investments. Here are some of the common mistakes made by most investors, beginners, and professional traders alike:

Failure to Understand the Trade

It is always wrong to invest in a trade or business you know nothing about. It is a great mistake to engage in stock trading when you do not understand the business and financial models involved. You can avoid this mistake by taking the time to research the stock market and stock trading before investing your money.

Know the different markets, the driving forces, as well as trading procedures. Most investors tend to buy stocks from the latest companies and industries they know very little about. Although such companies may look promising, it is difficult to determine whether they will continue to exist. Understanding a specific company gives you a better hand over other investors.

You will be able to make accurate predictions about the company or industry, which may bring you more profit. You will quickly tell when the business is booming, stagnating, or closing way before other investors get this information. Individuals who do not take time to study companies miss out on future trends of these companies. Failing to establish such trends leads to several missed opportunities. For instance, a person who invests in a company that is higher than his capital may quickly lose all his investment.

That is why it is always advisable that you invest in the industry you understand better. For instance, if you are a surgeon, you can invest in stocks that deal with medicine or related stocks. Lawyers can invest in companies that generate income through litigation, and so on.

Impatience

The stock market is for patient investors. It is a slow but steady form of investment. Although it bears various opportunities that can bring you money, you cannot make enough profit in one day. Most stock investors are always faced with the challenge of being patient. Some end up losing trade positions before they mature in the quest to make quick money. Exiting the market too early will always cost you some returns.

As a new investor, you must never expect your investment portfolio to perform more than its capability, as this will always lead to a disaster. Remain realistic in terms of the time, duration, and resources needed to earn from the market.

Failure to Diversify

Another mistake that easily causes disaster is the failure to diversify. Professional investors do not have a problem with this since they can easily profit from a single type of stock. However, young investors must be able to diversify to secure their investment. Some of them do not stick to this principle. Most of these lose a great fortune as soon as they get onto the stock market.

As you seek to invest, remember the rule of thumb governing stock diversity. This states that you should not invest more than 10% of your capital to one type of stock.

Getting Too Connected with a Certain Company

The essence of trading in stock is to make a profit. Sometimes, investors get too deep into a certain company that they forget that it is all about the shares and not the company itself.

Being too attached to a company may cloud your judgment when it comes to stock trading since you may end up buying stocks from this company instead of getting the best deal on the market. As you learn more about companies, always remember that you are into the business to make money, besides creating relationships.

Investment Turnover

Investment turnover refers to the act of entering and exiting positions at will. This is one other mistake that destroys great investments. It is only beneficial to institutions that seek to benefit from low commission rates. Most stock trading positions charge transaction fees.

The more frequent you buy and sell, the more you pay in terms of transaction fees. You, therefore, need to be careful when entering positions. Do not get in or exit too early. Have a rough idea of when you want to close positions so that you do not miss some of the long-term benefits of these positions.

Timing the Market

Market timing results in high investment turnover. It is not easy to successfully time the market. On average, only 94% of stock trading returns are acquired without the use of market timing. Most traders time the market as a way of attempting to recover their losses. They want to get even by making some profit to counter a loss. This is always known as a cognitive error in behavioral finance. Trying to get even on the stock market will always result in double losses.

Trading with Emotions

Allowing your emotions to rule is one of the things that kill your stock investment returns. Most people get into the market for fear of losses or thirst to make returns too fast. As a young trader, you must ensure that greed and fear do not overwhelm your decision making. Stock prices may fluctuate a lot in the short-term; however, this may not be the case in the long term, especially for large-cap stocks. This means that you may get lower profits in the short-term, but these may increase in the long-term.

Understanding this will help you avoid closing trades when it is not the right time yet.

Setting Unrealistic Expectations

This always occurs when dealing with small-cap stocks such as penny stocks. Most investors buy such stocks with the expectation that the prices will change drastically. Sometimes this works, but it is not a guarantee.

To make great fortunes, people invest a lot of capital on these stocks, and then the prices do not change much. If these investors are not prepared for such an eventuality, they may feel frustrated and may quit the business completely. However, this is something that you must be able to manage if you want to grow your investment. Do not expect more than what a certain type of stock can deliver.

Using Borrowed Money

This is probably one of the greatest mistakes that investors make. Some investors get carried away with the returns they are making. As a way of getting more profits, they borrow money and use it to enter more stock positions. This is a very dangerous move and can result in a lot of stress. Stock trading is like gambling. You are not always sure how much you take home at the end of each trade. It is therefore not advisable for you to invest borrowed money in it.

As you try to avoid these mistakes, you must also avoid getting information from the wrong sources. Some traders have lost a fortune because they relied on the wrong sources for stock information. It is important to isolate a small number of people and places where you will seek guidance from.

Do not be a person that follows the crowd. Take time before investing in new stock opportunities. Carry out proper due diligence, especially with small-cap stocks since these involve a lot of risks. Remember, you must trade carefully and implement expert advice if you want to succeed in stock trading.

In the stock market, every time someone buys another sells, both think they are smart.

Chapter 10.

Tips and Tricks for Successful Stocks Trading

Topic Covered:

- Always be Informed
- Buy Low, Sell High
- Scalping&Short Selling
- Identify the Pattern
- Look at the Results
- Look at the Company
- Don't Trust Mails

- Understand the Corrections
- Hire A Broker Only If Necessary
- Diversify Your Risks
- Money Movement
- Look at the Stock Volume

There are some tips and tricks that you can keep up your sleeve to help you invest in stocks. Let us look at some of them.

Always be Informed

You need to be informed about what happens in the market. This is the only way you can trust your decisions. You should go through different resources and publications if you want to obtain more information about the various stocks in the market.

Buy Low, Sell High

This is a strategy that most investors will use. It is always good to buy low and sell high, and you must follow this to the tee. It is when you do this that you can expect to make large profits in the market. When you buy low and sell high, you will purchase a stock at its lowest value and sell it at its highest value. It will be easy for you to determine when the stock price will reach the highest rate based on some methods and data you collect. You need to ensure that you always act according to the data that you have collected. Experts recommend that it is a good idea to buy stocks the minute the market opens. Most stocks reach their highest price in the afternoon, and that is when you should sell them.

Scalping

This is a very popular technique in the stock market. When you use this technique, you can always buy and sell stocks within a matter of a few seconds. Your purchases and sales depend on how fast you are. This is a very strange method, but it is very effective, especially in volatile markets. Let us assume that you purchased a stock at 10:00 AM and sold it at 10:02 AM The price of that stock is $3, and the selling price is $5. So, in a matter of two minutes, you made a $2 profit per share, and this is a great profit for a scalper. This does not seem like a profit, but if you do this at least twenty or thirty times a day, you can make a huge profit. You should only use this form of trading once you have enough experience in the market. If you want to take up this technique, you should have at least a year's worth of experience to help you make the right decisions.

Short Selling

Many traders use the concept of short selling when they invest in the market. Short selling refers to when you need to borrow stock from the holder and sell it to another buyer. Then, you will wait for the stock price to fall before you give the stocks back to the lender. This is one of the easiest ways in which you can capitalize on the volatility of the prices. You must make the right decisions about the investments you make and don't invest or borrow useless stocks. You must always ensure that you maintain a wide margin that will make a few mistakes. You should ensure that you have enough capital to support any other investments if things never work out. It is always good to buy shares back at the earliest if you believe that the price of the stocks will continue to increase.

Identify the Pattern

It is important to remember that stocks and every other stock in the market will follow a pattern. Once you notice this pattern and understand it, you can invest in stocks successfully. This pattern has all the information you need about the high and low points of the stocks and gathers some information on how you can trade between those points. It is important to have the history of the stock with you since it will help you determine the previous trend and predict the future trend of the stock.

Look at the Results

Every company is result-oriented, which means that the report published by the company will tell you how well the company is doing. The report that the company shares will shed some light on how well it is doing in the market. You should go through this report to ensure that you are making the right choice. The data collection results should show you that you could make enough profits when you invest in it. A small company will always aim to sell a large volume of stocks, and if you are impressed with the company and its numbers, you can invest in the stocks of that company. Remember that a company only publishes the results quarterly. Therefore, you need to look at all the results before you invest in the company.

Look at the Company Name

When choosing to invest in the stock market, you should understand that its name does matter. You must see if the company is well known and is doing well in the market. You can invest in a company that does not have any significant changes. Some people steer clear of such companies. If you are not a fundamentalist and are willing to take on a few risks, you can use technical analysis to help you make the decision. It is always good to learn more about the company if you choose to invest in shares in that company.

Understand the Company Better

You need to look at how the stock performs in the market, but it is important to spend some time understanding the company you are investing in. You need to know if the company is working on the right products and services. Understand the industry of the company. See if they are developing new products, technology, or services. Remember that whatever the company does affect the price of the stock. The best way for you to do this is to learn more about the company through fundamental analysis. You should always read the news about the company too. It is only this way that you can assess how well the company is doing. If you have any knowledge about the company or the products, you should spend some time to see where the company is heading.

When you start looking at a company, you need to ensure that you obtain the information from the right sources. Read this information carefully to understand whether the company is doing well or not. Ensure that the sources you use to obtain this information are reliable. If you get a fax, tip, or email from a person stating that one company is better than the rest, you need to make sure that you do not rush into investing. Take some time out and read about the company. Never invest in any company simply because of some information you may have received. Always conduct thorough research before you invest in the company. This is the only way you will learn if the company is doing well or not. Never waste your time or money. So, always stick to reliable sources and use that information to invest in the correct stocks.

Don't Trust Mails

You mustn't trust any emails that come from companies that claim to have enough knowledge about the stocks of other companies. These emails will also suggest the stocks that you should invest in, but the information in those emails is untrue. Companies cannot go through their investors' portfolios and suggest which stocks they should invest in. Even if a company does choose to do this, they may give you a suggestion that will not work for you. So, it is good to avoid these stocks and only invest in those stocks that you have all the information about.

Understand the Corrections

Remember that the price of stocks will be corrected in the market, and it is important that you remain patient. The price of the stock will drop when the market is correcting the price of the stocks in the market. If you are impatient, you will make a mistake and lose a lot of money. Always look at the company and make the right decisions about your investments. If a stock is either overpriced or underpriced, it means that the corrections will be made soon. Never sell your stocks in a panic and wait for the corrections to be made. You need to follow the news regularly, so you understand how or why the correction is being made.

Hire a Broker Only if Necessary

You should never hire a broker to do the job for you unless you need one. The only reason is that a broker will charge you a fee for helping you with your investments. They will also ask you to pay a commission, which will eat into your profits. You also need to remember that you need to pay your broker a fee regardless of whether you make a profit. So, they do not have to work hard to ensure that you make a profit. There are theories that companies hire brokers to increase the price of the stock in the market. They request the brokers to motivate investors to trade in a specific stock even if they do not want to invest in that stock. You will purchase these stocks if you can be swayed easily, which will lead to huge losses. You should always look for discounts online and see if you can trade independently. Avoid depending on your broker to buy and sell your stock.

Diversify Your Risks

This has been mentioned repeatedly across the book, so you can imagine how important it is for you to do this. You must always diversify your risks depending on the type of investment you make. This holds for any instrument. When you choose to invest in stocks, try to invest in stocks from different industries and sectors. If you invest in stocks only in one sector, you will lose a lot of money if the industry were to crash. It is because of this that you need to ensure that you diversify your capital. You must invest in different instruments in the market. Yes, one industry may be doing well compared to other industries, but this does not mean that you put all your money on stocks in that industry.

Money Movement

If you notice a sudden change in the price movement and the flow of money in the company, you know that the stock value will increase. If there is a sudden increase in the capital through external sources or it pumped its profits into its business, then it means that the company wants to expand. This will mean that the stock prices will rise, and it will benefit you as an investor. You must always keep track of the news and make the right decisions.

Look at the Stock Volume

If you notice that the volume of the stock has suddenly changed in the market, it is always a good idea to invest in that stock. The sudden changes in the price and volume of the stock will happen when there is some information in the news about the stock that makes people buy or sell stocks. Ensure that you capitalize on these situations so that you can make a huge profit. According to Timothy Sykes, you should always purchase a stock if you experience a high price after one year. The price of the stock will change only when the company talks about its earnings and bonuses.

Chapter 11.

Stock Exchange Terms

Topic Covered:

- Annual Report, Arbitrage
- Averaging Down
- Bear&Bull Markets
- Bid, Close, Open, Order and Execution
- Day trading

- Dovodend
- Exchange
- High&Low
- Initial Public Offering
- Leverage & Margin
- Moving Average

If you are planning to start investing your money in the stock market, then there are some common stock exchange terms that you must know. These terms are essential in understanding the behavior of the stock market. You should also have known the basics before diving onto the live trade. These terms will help you achieve your goals and build your career in the stock market to become a successful trader.

Stock exchange terms are slang specifically for industry security. Professionals and expert traders use these terms to talk about different game plans, patterns, charts, and many other related elements of the stock market industry. Common stock exchange terms are listed below:

Annual Report

The company specifically makes the yearly report of its shareholders. This report is designed in such a way that it attracts the shareholders. The annual report carries all the information about the company's shares and their game plan for the present and future. When you are going through the annual report, you gather information about the company's financial situation.

Arbitrage

This is one of the most advanced terms in the stock market, which every trader should know. This refers to buying stocks at a low price from one market and selling at a higher rate on another market.

For example, sometimes a stock ABC trade on 50$ on one market and the same stock on the other market trade on 55$ so traders buy shares on low price points and sell them on higher rates to make the profit.

Averaging Down

When stock prices fall, and you plan to buy stocks on lower rates, your average buying prices decrease. This strategy is used most commonly in the stock market. After buying, you plan to sell those stocks shares when the stock market rebounds.

Bear Market

A bear market is opposite to Bull market. It means that the overall market is negative or falling. In this stage, the market falls up to 20% the quarter after quarter. This is one of the scariest situations for big investors because their investments are at great risk.

Bull Market

Bull Market is opposite to the bear market. Bull market meant the rising of the stock points. In this stage, people start investing money in the stock market because of their positive behavior.

Beta

This is the whole relationship between the stocks and the overall market. If stock ABC has a beta of 5.5 means that every one-point movement in the market, the stock ABC moves 5.5 points and vice versa.

Bourse

In short, Bourse is a modern and more advanced name of the stock market. It means where people gather for the purchasing and selling of stock shares. Most commonly, it refers to Paris stock exchanges or non-US stock exchanges.

Broker

Many people who are beginners and don't understand the behavior of the stock market contact different brokers. These brokers are experienced traders who have sound knowledge of trading of stocks. These beginners contact these brokers and ask them to buy and sell stocks for them. Brokers charge high commissions for these services.

Bid

Bidding is as common and simple as we do in freelancing and other daily projects. In stock market, the bidder—who is a buyer—gives an offer for a specific share. Bid means the buyer willing to buy the share on his desired rates. The bid is made according to the asking price of the seller.

Close

Simply this refers to the time when trading will stop, and the stock market will close. Its timings vary from country to country. Each stock market has its own time of closing and opening. After closing the stock market, it is not available for live trade.

Day trading

This is one of the most advanced terms in the stock market. Day trading refers to buying and selling of stocks shares on the same day. Many experienced traders use this method.

After buying shares, people wait for the following day to sell them at much higher rates. But there are 50/50 chances that they may end up with profit or loss. So, Day trading is a smart strategy, but it requires a lot of experience to make profits.

Dividend

Many companies offer incentives to attract more traders to their company. Some companies pay their shareholders one of their earnings portions, which are called the dividend. Some companies pay dividends annually or quarterly. Not all companies offer a dividend.

Exchange

Exchange refers to a place where thousands of investments are traded daily. There are many popular exchanges in the world. New York Stock Exchange is one of the most popular exchanges, which is present in the United States of America.

Execution

We are familiar with this term in the sense of computer where it means the completion of a task. In the stock market, it also acts the same as in the said case. When a trader buys or sells stock shares, after completion, it is said that the transaction has been executed.

Haircut

The haircut is the most known term used in the stock market. There is a slight difference between the buyer's bid and the asking price of the seller.

High

High indicates the milestone reached by the stocks. It points out that the specific stock has never reached such a high price before. In the stock market, there is also one other high. This high is used to demonstrate the milestone reached by stocks in a specific period. It may be fortnightly or in 30 days.

Initial Public Offering

Initial Public Offering means that when a company decides to expand its business and offers its stocks available for the public. The Securities Exchange Commissions is responsible for issuing Initial Public offering and is very strict against its rules.

Leverage

Leverage is considered the riskiest and dangerous game tom plays in the stock market. After having your complete research, you decide to borrow shares from your broker and set up a plan to sell them on higher rates. If you successfully sell those shares on higher rates, you again return those borrowed shares to the broker and keep the difference.

Low

Low is opposite to high. It indicates that the specific stocks have never fallen to this price before. Low is also demonstrated for a specific period may be weekly or monthly.

Margin

Margin is almost the same as that of leverage. It is also considered one of the riskiest games. It is an account that allows you to borrow money from the broker to invest that money into the stocks. Now the difference between the loan which you borrowed from the broker and rates of the securities is called margin.

Margin is not for beginners; even the most experienced traders fail to apply this strategy.

Moving Average

It is the average price of the stock shares at a specific time. 50 and 200 are considered the best common time frames to study the behavior of the moving average.

Open

Simply refers to the time when the stock market is open for the live trade. Traders start buying and selling of stocks according to their plans. This varies from country to country. Every stock market has its own time to open and close.

Order

Order is the same as bid, but in the order, you decide to buy or sell stock shares according to your plan after deciding your order to sell or buy the stocks. For example, if you are willing to buy 200 shares, then you must make an order.

Pink Sheet Stocks

Many beginners take start with pink sheet stocks. If you are just planning to invest in this stock market, you probably have listened to pink sheet stocks. These are penny stocks and are traded on a small scale, and each share price is 5$ or even less than that. Because these are the shares of smaller companies, you will not find them on the big markets such as New York Stock Exchange.

Sector

Dozens of companies belong to the same industry. These companies are available publicly on the stock market to buy their shares. These stocks groups which belong to the same industry are called sectors. There are many advantages to investing in the same sector because it is much easy to predict the fluctuations.

BONUS CHAPTER:
How to Use the Indicators

Candlesticks and eyeballing charts to spot trend lines, support, and resistance are all very useful. These are subjects that you should study very carefully if you intend to become a trader. However, you'll need to add 2-3 indicators to your tool bag if you expect to become a successful trader. Indicators help take the noise out from stock market data and help you do things like get a dynamic representation of the standard deviation in price ranges for the stock. This can help confirm signals that you are seeing from the candles or in your trend analysis and these tools can also help you identify the best entry and exit points for your trades. We begin with a discussion of moving average.

Moving Average

Stock market data is noisy. You can instantly make out the noise on any line chart of stock prices. It's very jagged, and seems random. If you want to analyze the data and get an accurate view of where it's headed and what kind of price ranges the stock is going to have in the near future, it would be helpful to smooth out the curve. To pick out trends, it would also be helpful to look at curves that rely on more recent data and compare them to curves containing long-term data.

This is what the moving average does. You know what an average is. A simple average means you simply add up some data points and then divide by the number of points. So for example, we can average the test scores in a class with six students:

55, 67, 71, 78, 86, 94

The average is just:

Average = (55 + 67 + 71 +78 +86 +94)/6 = 75.2

A moving average is an average of data in a time series that moves along with the data, by a fixed number of periods. Suppose that for the first 10 days of July the high temperature was:

87, 88, 85, 90, 92, 87, 93, 95, 97, 94

The average is:

Average = (87 + 88 + 85 + 90 + 92 + 87 + 93 + 95 + 97 + 94)/10 = 90.8

A moving average calculates the average at each given point. It's defined in part by the number of time periods or periods used for the average. So we could have a 3 period average, which means at each point it would calculate the average of the three most recent data points. We could start a moving average calculation for our temperature data on day 3:

Moving average at day 3 = (85 + 88 +87)/3 = 86.7

Then you re-calculated it at each point, moving over one step. The moving average on day 4 is:

Moving average at day 4 = (90 + 85 + 88)/3 = 87.7 Then on day 5 it would be:

Moving average at day 5 = (92 + 90 + 85)/3 = 89

This type of moving average is called a simple moving average. It calculates the simple average at each data point. This is a common type of moving average used to analyze stock market trends. You can compute moving averages using different numbers of periods. Some commonly used moving averages are 9-period, 20-period, 50-period, and 200-period. The period can be any period used in your analysis, swing traders often use days.

It produces a smoothed out curve of the pricing data in the stock market. In the chart below, we see how a 10-day moving average produces a nice, smooth curve that flows along the general trend of the stock market pricing data.

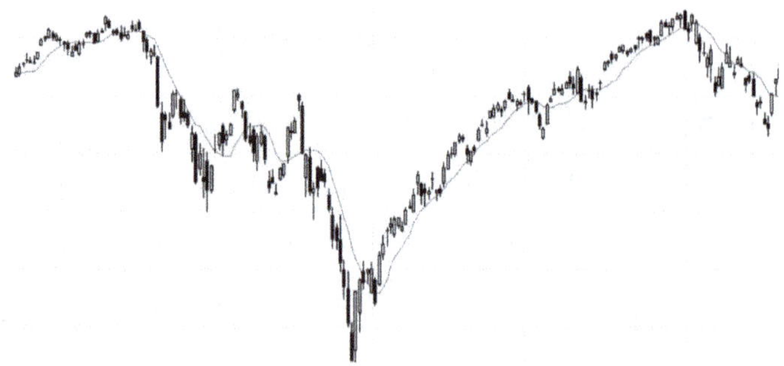

One thing you'll notice about the simple moving average is that it's got some accuracy problems, despite the overall fairly good fit of the curve. At some points, it can lag the data.

Weighted Moving Averages

A major criticism of the simple moving average is that it gives equal weight to distant prices and recent prices. In fact any data in the moving average calculation has the same weight as any other. I am sure that you will agree that it's more likely that recent prices are going to be more influential on the trend. Market sentiment 10 days ago isn't as influential as market sentiment today, yesterday, or the past three days.

For this reason many weighted moving averages have been developed. The most frequently used weighted moving average is the exponential moving average. It was developed using a complicated formula that helps make the data more relevant. You don't need to bother with knowing the formula behind the exponential moving average. The only thing you need to know about it is that it gives the prices from more recent trading sessions more weight than it gives prices from 5, 10, or more trading sessions ago. This helps make the curve more accurate.

There are other more advanced moving averages that can be used for indicators, although it's debatable whether or not they are very useful or not. Many traders even stick to using simple moving averages, and exponential moving averages tend to be the most popular among traders operating over shorter time frames. Exponential moving averages have a lot of popularity on the Forex markets.

You can calculate the moving average using different data. The most commonly used metric is the closing price of each trading session. However, you can use the opening price as well. Other options include the high price, the low price, or fractions of each.

It's also possible to calculate moving averages based on volume of trading. That can be very useful information, since volume of trading can correspond to real price movements on the markets.

In the chart section displayed below, we've shown two moving averages, one in thick black and one in thin black. The moving average in thin black is an exponential moving average, while the thick black curve is a simple moving average. I'd like to call your attention to the fact that the simple moving average curve lags the change, as seen by the dip in share prices toward the right hand side. It's more accurately tracked by the exponential moving average.

Crossings to forecast trend reversals

The most important information that an indicator can give you is forecasting a trend reversal.

In order to forecast trend reversals, you'll use two moving average curves of the same type but with different periods on your stock chart. The focus is on what short term pricing is doing with respect to the average pricing for the given stock you are looking at.

A trend reversal is indicated when the short period moving average crosses the long period moving average. If the short period moving average crosses above the long period moving average, this indicates a coming upward trend in price. On the other hand if the short period moving average crosses below the long period moving average, this indicates a coming downward trend in price.

The following chart shows this effect, comparing a 9 period moving average (in thin black) to a 50 period moving average, thick black. The moving averages in this case are simple moving averages. One thing to notice is that while the crossings do indicate trend reversals, simple moving averages tend to lag the actual pricing data.

Starting from the left hand side, while the short period moving average follows the data fairly well, notice that the downtrend in prices takes place before the short period moving average crosses below the long period moving average. Note that the candlesticks gave strong indication of a downward pressure in prices before the crossing of the moving averages took place.

A similar phenomenon is visible moving from left to right across the chart. Notice that in the center there is a mild uptrend in prices, but there is no crossing of the moving averages that is evident. By the time the short period moving average crosses above the long period moving average, the upward trend that starts a bit past the end of the final major downturn in prices was already well underway.

However, we observe a similar situation using the 50-period exponential moving average together with a 9-period exponential moving average. Again, the prominent upward trend in the right section of the chart is well underway long before the crossing of the curves occurs. If you were relying on the moving average indicators, you would have missed quite a bit of significant price movement – so you would have erred in deciding when the best time to enter the trade was.

Comparing shorter period moving averages for more accuracy

We can get a much better handle on the trends by using a shorter period moving average. Instead of using a 50-period moving average, we can compare a 20-period moving average against a 9-period moving average. Now you'll see that the cross overs indicate a trend reversal far earlier.

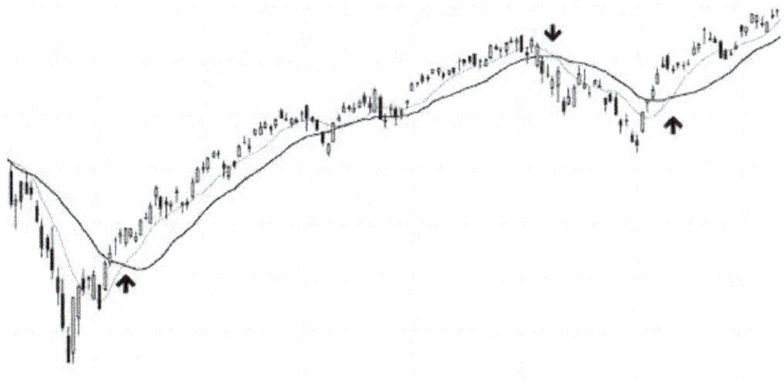

That may not be surprising. You have to ask how relevant a 50 period moving average is when looking for trend reversals in the present day. Even the example shown here – which is far better and so would help you capture a lot more of the pricing gain – the price moved from $274 a share to $283 a share before the crossover on the right side occurred. On the other hand, the large bullish candle that starts the uptrend is a pretty clear indicator.

This example clearly demonstrates how tricky this type of analysis can be. It also illustrates why you can't rely on one indicator alone. The candles also prove their worth yet again, and despite problems with the candles, especially recently, they remain one of the most accurate forecasting tools available to the trader.

It turns out going to shorter period moving averages won't help much. You'd still be at $283 a share up from $274 a share if you waited for the crossover of the moving averages in order to enter a position, losing out on $9 in price appreciation. A trader using candles however wouldn't have missed out.

Heightened accuracy using Hull moving averages

When you use Hull moving averages instead, you're going to find that the cross overs are far more accurate. In fact, in the case of the Hull moving averages, you will often see crossovers before they are indicated by the candles. In the chart below, we use a 9-period Hull moving average together with a 20-period Hull moving average. Notice that this time, we don't miss out on any of the price gains, if we used the crossover as our guideline to enter the trade.

Let's zoom in, so that you can clearly see the crossover of the Hull moving averages happens before the candlesticks indicate an upward trend.

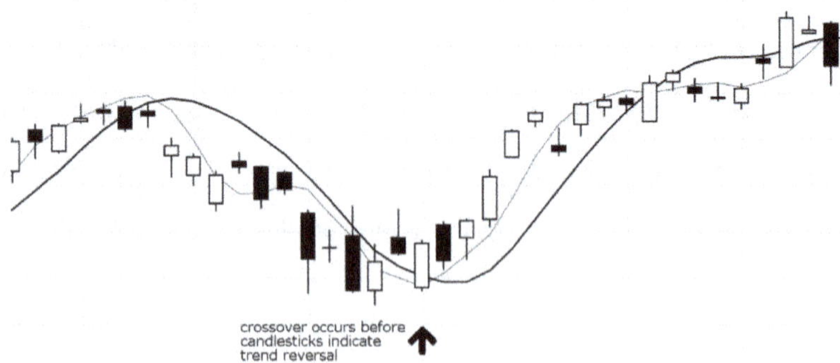

Golden Cross

A golden cross occurs when the short-term moving average crosses above the long-term moving average. To look for a golden cross, most traders compare the 50-period moving average to a longer-term 200-period moving average. If these moving averages indicate a trend reversal, it is a strong signal that the stock may be heading into a rally.

A golden cross is considered to be a breakout pattern. That is, the stock may have been fluctuating within a certain range of prices for some time. During that period it would reach high prices, but they would not break above a resistance price level or go very far above it. And in each case, the price would drop back down. Price may then drop down to a lower support price level. A breakout is when the stock finally breaks above resistance and begins a longer term upward trend. The upward trend signals a rally and it can last for long time periods.

When applied to major stock indexes like the S & P 500 (or using an exchange traded fund like SPY that tracks it as a proxy), a golden cross can be taken as an indicator of a bull market. If you are looking for trends during a recession or bear market, you may be interested in the ability to forecast when the market has hit bottom. After that point, the market will begin a new rally and we can consider that the bear market has come to an end. While it's certainly not a guarantee, a golden cross is a strong indicator of a coming bull market. It can be helpful to compare the major indexes or their proxies in exchange traded funds, such as the Dow Jones Industrial Average, NASDAQ and other market segments such as the RUT (Russell 2000).

For an individual stock, a golden cross is a strong buy signal if you are looking to go long on the stock and take advantage of a major price swing.

Death Cross

The death cross is the opposite condition when compared to a golden cross. In this case, you look for a short-term moving average to cross below a long-term moving average. When looking for a death cross, the 50-period moving average and the 200-period moving average are the best time periods to use for this purpose. Therefore, with a death cross you are looking for the 50-period moving average to cross below the 200-period moving average.

While a golden cross can signal a long-term (in relative, or absolute terms) price increase, a death cross signals a coming long-term drop in prices. If you are long on the position now is a good time to sell your stock. If you are looking to short the stock, a death cross is a good entry point.

We can also look for a death cross when studying the major indexes of the markets. A death cross for the Dow Jones Industrial Average or the S & P 500 can be a strong signal of a coming bear market.

Relative Strength Index (RSI)

Every trader should include the relative strength index in their analysis.

This helps you determine the momentum of a trend. The range of the RSI is 0 to 100, and it's shown as a graph below your stock chart. The RSI is known as a momentum oscillator.

The relative strength index helps you determine if a stock is overbought or oversold. If a stock is overbought, the price has reached an unjustifiably high level. That means the price has gone above the intrinsic value of the stock. You can check fundamentals like the price to earnings ratio to help determine this as well.

With traders and investors now paying too much for the stock, they are going to start pulling back. This can lead to a downward trend in prices. An RSI that is signaling overbought conditions often correlates with continued uptrends that quickly pull back. There is no longer enough buyer interest in the stock to keep pushing prices higher.

The condition used to determine if a stock is overbought is an RSI that goes over 70. If you have bought shares hoping to profit from an upward trend in price, this is a good indicator that it's a good time to sell your shares, or that you should sell your shares in the near future. When a stock is in overbought conditions, it's not typically going to stay at the high price level for very long.

During a strong uptrend in price, the RSI can range between 40-90. You can look at the RSI chart and use the same chart analysis you do for stock charts. That is you should look for patterns like head and shoulders and double tops that indicate a coming price reversal. These often show up on an RSI chart while failing to appear on the stock chart itself.

An important pattern to look for when doing your momentum analysis is a so-called failure swing. When there is a failure swing the price of the stock moves up to a higher price, and then drops down to a previous, temporary line of support. This might happen more than once. The key characteristic of a failure swing is that there is not enough upward momentum in the stock to push the price past a certain point.

The RSI can be used to confirm a general trend in stock prices as well, if it's above 40 but less than 70, this indicates enough momentum to keep an upward trend going. When your other indicators and candles are all signaling uptrend, you can confirm the strength and momentum of the uptrend by using the RSI. You can ride the uptrend until the RSI reaches a value in the range 70-90.

RSI doesn't also tell you the momentum for trends or signal price reversals, you can also use it to help establish a price level of support. If you are seeing what appears to be support in the charts, confirm with the RSI. Levels of 40-45 indicate pricing support for the relative strength index. A level of resistance can be found if the RSI is anywhere in the range of 65-75 and it goes along in this range for sometime without increasing. Confirm with what you're seeing on the stock chart itself.

Look for downward trends in the peaks reached by the RSI in the same manner that you would when looking at charts. If the RSI reaches some peak value and drops only to rise again, but fails to reach the first peak without entering a new decline, this is a strong signal of a coming price reversal. Again, these patterns may appear on the RSI without showing up on the stock chart. Do not dismiss them even though they are not showing up on the stock charts, this is a strong indicator of changing momentum.

When it comes to downward trends in pricing, if the relative strength index falls below 30 this can indicate oversold conditions. Now the stock is becoming undervalued and a price reversal can be imminent. This is a strong signal that indicates it's a good time to enter a position, if you are going long on the stock. Resistance can be indicated when the RSI won't drop below 20 during a downtrend.

If there is a very strong uptrend, seeing an indication of overbought conditions should not be taken as an automatic sell signal. Prices can often continue with an upward trend in overbought conditions for some time. Remember that people do not always act in rational ways. On the stock market, greed can set in and people will be overcome by excitement and exuberance, hoping to see ever-higher prices. There are also latecomers to any uptrend. These two factors can sometimes lead to a continuing uptrend even though the RSI is telling you there are overbought conditions. In this situation, you should seek confirmation from other signals before using the overbought conditions as a reason to exit your position.

The same logic applies to downtrends. There may be an indication of oversold conditions, but emotion can take hold and rule the day here as well. As investors start panicking, and they see other investors exiting their positions to avoid what they mistakenly believe to be a catastrophic crash in stock prices, more will join the selloff and cause prices to continue going lower for some period of time. Therefore, as you should be doing in the case of uptrends, confirm what you are seeing with the RSI by looking at other tools. This can include looking for crossovers in your moving averages, examining chart patterns, and keeping a close eye on candles.

Swing failures occur at price peaks when the stock reaches high prices and then breaks down to a new low before increasing again for a short time period. This is taken as a strong signal of changing momentum, and it's a good time to exit a long position – you've probably gotten as much profit out of the trend as you can get at this point. This is called a Top Swing Failure. So you will look for the price to rise to a peak, then drop down to a low value we will call A. Then the stock will rise again, this time probably reaching a peak price that is a little bit lower than the previous peak, only to drop to a new low price B, before rising again. The key piece of data to confirm a Top Swing Failure is if B < A.

Swing failures occur at the bottom of downtrends as well, indicating that a selloff is running out of momentum. This is called a Bottom Swing Failure. Here we simply look for the opposite pattern to that described in the last paragraph. In this situation, the price declines to a new low price A, and then pushes against the trend over a short time period to reach a high point C. The price then reverses and falls to a low price B. If B > A and the price starts rising again to C, this is considered a Bottom Swing Failure and indicates a price reversal into an uptrend.

Bollinger Bands

One of the most useful indicators in technical analysis are the Bollinger Bands. Bollinger bands combine three useful pieces of data into a single indicator. Bollinger bands include the moving average, a lower boundary curve determined by the moving one or more standard deviations below the average, and an upper boundary curve determined by going one or more standard deviations above the average.

Typically, Bollinger bands are used with a 20-period simple moving average. This will be the central line seen on the charts. For the standard deviation, it's common to use two standard deviations to set the upper and lower boundary curves. An example is shown below.

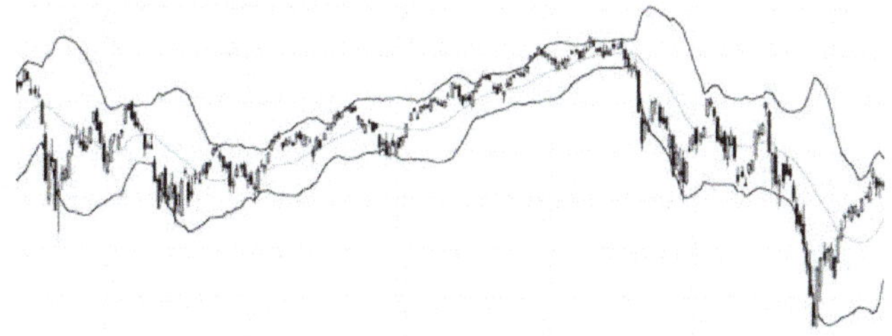

Bollinger bands, like the RSI, can be used to determine whether or not a stock is entering overbought or oversold conditions. When prices fall outside of the two standard deviation range, this is taken to be a strong signal of a price reversal. That doesn't mean, by itself, that a breakout is coming. It may only mean that the price will revert back to the mean. In the above image, we see both conditions. You can note in the image several points where the price reverted back to the mean, but there is a strong uptrend slightly to the right of the center of the figure.

Notice that the strength of the trend can usually – but not always be confirmed with candles. In the figure the point where there was a shift from the lower Bollinger band to the upper Bollinger band with a strong uptrend, there is a gap between the candles and the second candle after reading the bottom of the downtrend is a strong bullish candle.

The Bollinger bands can be taken to be dynamic representations of support and resistance price levels for the stock. This is seen clearly in the figure.

Although it's not particularly useful in this case, since the particular security used (SPY) went though a significant downtrend followed by a significant up trend, using the Bollinger bands as a guideline in a ranging market is particularly useful. A ranging market is one where prices are staying within relatively fixed levels of support and resistance for a prolonged time period.

When using Bollinger bands, traders look for "tagging". This happens when the wicks of the candles touch or go outside one of the bands. It's considered that you should use a candle as a signal of a price change when it goes with the trend but there is a tagging indicator. As an example, you would look for a bearish candle at the peak of an uptrend that tags or even goes outside the Bollinger band all together.

It's important to use other signals and not rely on Bollinger bands in isolation. For example, during a long uptrend you will often see prices rise a small amount and then drop a little, forming a hump shape, before rising to a higher level. These small price humps can occur as part of a larger uptrend. Mistaking a hump for a peak because it touches or goes outside a Bollinger band can be a major mistake, causing you to miss out on further price increases for the stock.

It's common to put two sets of Bollinger bands on the same stock chart. In this case, a one-standard deviation set of Bollinger bands is included with the two-standard deviation set. The trader can then look for pricing trends where prices stay in between the one and two standard deviation zone.

If this takes place during what appears to be an uptrend, the zone in between the two standard deviations is taken to be a "buying zone" where traders looking to enter long positions can do so (that is buy the stock in hopes of price appreciation).

Likewise, when prices are staying in the lower range that is they are largely confined between one standard deviation below the mean and two standard deviations below the mean, this would be a "selling zone". This is a signal indicating a downward trend in prices. Alternatively, a short seller would use a buying zones as an indication to exit a position, or if they are not already in a position to wait for the price to show signs of peaking. Likewise, a selling zone is a buying zone for those shorting the stock.

The example below illustrates a selling zone, and you can see the downward trend. The grey zone indicates one-standard deviation, while the white zone indicates two-standard deviations, and you can see that for a significant amount of time the share prices are falling in between the two, forming a good example of a selling zone.

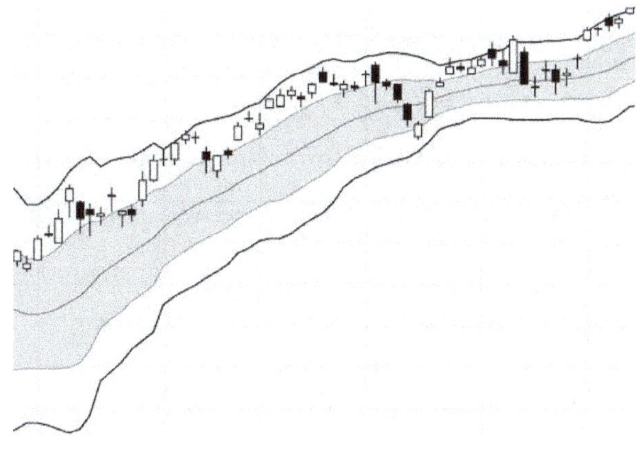

This example shows a buying zone. Prices for the most part are within the 1-2 standard deviation range.

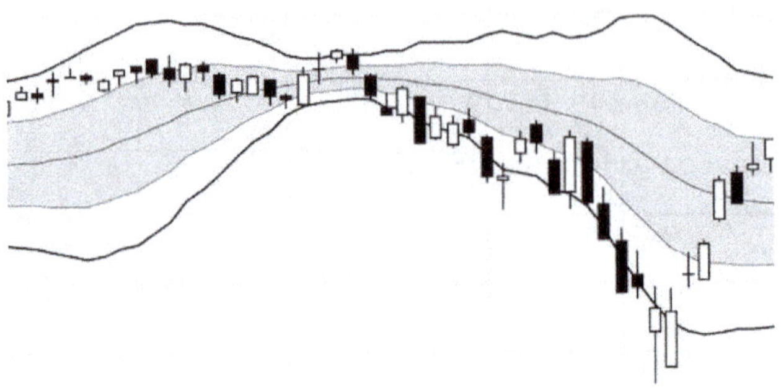

Volatility and Bollinger Bands

The volatility of a stock is closely tied to the size of the standard deviation at any given time. Taking this into account, we recognize that Bollinger bands can be used to measure or estimate the volatility of a stock at any given moment or observe how it's changing with time. Remember that volatility is a measure of the magnitude of price swings for the stock. That is, if stock A ranges between $50 and $55 with a mean of $53 over the course of a week, but stock B ranges between $40 and $60 with a mean of $50 over the course of a week, we'd consider stock B to be more volatile. High volatility implies larger and more frequent price swings over a given period of time. More volatility is going to result in a larger standard deviation. In the case of Bollinger bands this is represented visually by the width of the Bollinger bands.

When volatility is getting larger, the Bollinger bands are going to be wider. When volatility is decreasing or smaller, the Bollinger bands are going to be narrow. Small adjustments in the standard deviation used are suggested for longer and shorter periods used with the moving average. A two standard deviation width is the default value used with a 20-period moving average. If the moving average is longer, then it's recommended that the standard deviation be slightly increased. For a 50-period moving average, it is advised that you use a 2.1 standard deviation width. On the other hand, for a shorter period moving average, you should slightly decrease the standard deviation. In the case of a 10-period moving average, it's advised that you use 1.9 standard deviations. Below, we see a chart for Apple, using a 10-period moving average and 1.9 standard deviations for the Bollinger bands.

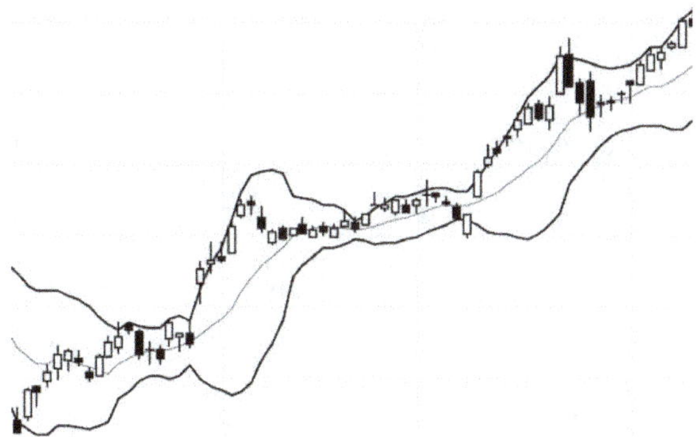

The W bottom and M top pattern in Bollinger Bands

One key thing to look for with Bollinger bands are patterns that show a reversal back to the mean, either at the bottom of a downtrend or at the top of an uptrend. These can indicate a coming trend reversal. At the bottom of a downtrend, a W bottom is indicated by a price drop that hits the lower Bollinger band, then prices reverse back to the mean. Then it drops a second time, again reaching the lower Bollinger band. Once again price reverses and starts increasing again. If it reaches the median a second time, this is a W bottom. That is a strong indicator that the price will continue rising forming an uptrend above the mean.

An M top works in the reverse. This time prices rise from the mean and peak when hitting the upper Bollinger band, only to revert back to the mean. Then they rise again, but can't break through the top pricing level, so prices stop rising at the upper Bollinger band and then reverse, going back down to the mean. This is usually followed by a downtrend in prices below the mean and perhaps beyond.

Band Walking

It's important to recognize that when prices touch or even go slightly outside the Bollinger bands, that in itself isn't a buy or sell signal. It needs to be confirmed by looking at other metrics and signals, including crosses of moving averages and looking at the candles themselves. Price trends also do what traders refer to as "walk the band".

This means that a long string of prices will touch the band without a trend reversal. This can happen when the price is following an upward trend or when the price is declining.

Moving Average Convergence – Divergence

This indicator is another "momentum oscillator". It utilizes two exponential moving averages. But rather than just plotting them on a chart, it calculates their difference. The standard is to subtract a longer period moving average from a short period moving average, and this is normally done with a 12-period EMA (exponential moving average) and a 26-period EMA. The difference between the two curves is called the MACD line.

But that isn't all that is included with this indicator. It also includes a curve which is called the signal line. The signal line is calculated by computing the 9-day exponential moving average of the MACD line. The results are then used to look for buy and sell signals. Traders seek points where the MACD line crosses above and below the signal line. If it crosses above the signal line, using a standard bullish perspective, that is taken to be a buy signal. Therefore, if you are hoping to profit from a price swing that leads to appreciation of the stock price, you are looking for the MACD line to cross above the signal line. Conversely, if the MACD line crosses below the signal line, this is taken to be a sell signal for those who are bullish on the stock. On the other hand, if you are shorting the stock or buying put options, this is your point to enter the trade. Since the MACD line is calculated by subtracting one moving average from another, it can have positive and negative values. It's going to be positive when the 12 period exponential moving average is above the 26 period exponential moving average. In addition to giving buy and sell signals, the MACD gives you a measure of the momentum of a pricing trend. The MACD is usually displayed below stock charts with a histogram which gives a bar chart representation of the difference between the two moving averages.

The MACD has been criticized for not always being accurate, so it is not something a trader should come to rely on 100% of the time. It will often miss trend reversals and can give signals of a price uptrend or downtrend that will fail to materialize. Many traders study market momentum looking at the MACD and the RSI together. In any case, if you use the MACD to do technical analysis, it is recommended that you utilize other tools with it, and don't take the MACD alone for a buy or sell signal. Always confirm with other indicators.

Parabolic Stop and Reverse (SAR)

The parabolic stop and reverse or SAR indicator is a simple trend indicator. It appears on stock charts as a series of dots or dashes, that fall below or above the actual prices. When the parabolic stop and reverse curve is above prices, that indicates the market is in a downtrend. When it's below prices that indicates that the market is in an uptrend.

Therefore, traders look for the parabolic stop and reverse to change its appearance above or below prices. If you purchased shares of stock at the bottom of an uptrend, then you would watch for the parabolic stop and reverse curve data points to start showing up above prices as a sell indicator. Alternatively, someone looking to short the stock at that point would use that as a signal to enter their trade.

The parabolic stop and reverse indicator isn't useful in a ranging market. It's useful when the stock breaks out into a trend, and it can be helpful when other indicators are giving confusing signals.

ADX

ADX stands for average directional index. This is another oscillator that can give you a measure of the strength of a trend in market prices.

Despite its name, it actually doesn't give the direction of any trend, it only tells you if it's a strong or a weak trend. This is an important distinction, because many indicators simply give buy and sell or trend reversal signals. The range of the ADX is from 0 to 100. To look for a strong trend (regardless of direction), you are looking for the ADX to be above 50.

If the ADX is 20 or below, this is considered a weak trend. That means it lacks momentum and not many traders and investors are behind the trend.

You will remember that the MACD can give some false positives. You can utilize the ADX with the MACD and other indicators to help weed out false positives. There is no question this has applications when using the MACD, but you can also use the ADX with any indicators you are relying on to forecast trends. It can act as a double check to indicate whether or not entering or exiting a position is really a good move.

The ADX is good to check when you have been riding a trend to the upside. It will help you see when the trend is weakening, even though prices may be continuing to increase. This may be a reasonable point to exit the trade.

The Stochastic Indicator

In mathematics, the word stochastic refers to a random process. The stock market is certainly infused with a great deal of randomness. So it's natural that getting a handle on it is the basis for an important indicator. The stochastic indicator is considered to be a highly accurate indicator by the trading community.

The stochastic indicator seeks to determine the relationship between the current price and the price range of the stock over a period of time. Like some other indicators, it can be used to determine if a stock is overbought or oversold. The stochastic indicator uses 14 time periods, but it's flexible. It can use days, weeks, or months, so is useful to all styles of trading. That means you can zoom in and out, viewing 14 days, or 14 months. The stochastic indicator uses a fundamental observation, which you can see from candlesticks. That is the closing price of a stock tends to be in the upper range of prices for the trading session, when the stock is in an uptrend. Conversely, when the stock is in a downtrend, the closing price tends to be in the low range of stock prices for the trading session.

The stochastic indicator determines the stock's high and low price over a given period of time. It can then compare the current price to the range defined by the high and low, and express that as a percentage.

The stochastic indicator ranges over 0 to 100. If it's below 30, this is taken to indicate oversold conditions, and so it's a buy signal. Over 70 represents overbought conditions, and so would be a value indicating a sell signal. Anything in between 30 and 70 should be ignored.

Stochastic Momentum

The stochastic momentum index is a more sophisticated version of the stochastic indicator that is used to seek out oversold and overbought conditions. The indicator is supposed to provide an accurate forecast of coming shifts in momentum.

This indicator focuses on the high and low prices of each trading session, and uses them to calculate the median price value. It then calculates the difference between the closing price of each trading session and the median price. The purpose of developing this indicator was to avoid false buy and sell signals that resulted from false price swings. It ranges from -100 to +100.

When you set up the stochastic momentum index on a stock chart, you'll be asked to specify overbought and oversold ranges. The standard values are +40 for overbought conditions and -40 for oversold conditions. Therefore an indicator value of +42 would be overbought and an indicator value of -42 would be oversold.

Like the ordinary stochastic indicator, the stochastic momentum index does not tell you the coming trend, it only tells you there is going to be a shift in momentum. The trader has to get the trend direction using other tools. The main use of the stochastic momentum index is to help traders decide when to make their trades.

The indicator line is denoted by the obscure symbol %K, so when you set it up and it asks you for the number of periods for %K, it's asking you for the number of periods to use for the indicator. The standard value that is used is 10 periods, so if you are using days for your trading sessions, %K will be 10 days. The signal line is given by %D, with a standard period of 10. The signal line is an exponential moving average (it's a simple moving average for the regular stochastic indicator). The trader looks for line crossings. A downward crossing of the indicator line below the signal line is a bearish signal, while an upward crossing is taken to be a bullish signal.

Indicators – A Summary

A trader should never rely on any single indicator or chart pattern to enter or exit a trade. Instead, you should develop a practice of using a few specific tools. There are many more tools available, this description is only introductory and gives you an overview of the most common tools that are used. The key is to avoid jumping off and sinking a large amount of capital into a trade just because one indicator gave you a "go" signal. Likewise, you should avoid a premature exit from your positions by again only relying on a single indicator.

Many indicators are redundant. So, a Hull moving average and an exponential moving average with their crossover signals are going to provide the same information. In that case, you should experiment with the different moving averages and find on moving average that works for you. Checking across multiple moving averages is simply beating a dead horse.

As a trader, you should definitely be a master of the candlesticks. That means being able to eyeball the candlesticks to spot probable trend reversals. They can also help you get an idea of momentum in a trend or toward a reversal. Candlestick chart analysis should be used in conjunction with moving averages.

Beyond this, you should utilize one or more of the other indicators described in this chapter. For example, using the relative strength index to determine when a trend you're looking at is getting into overbought or oversold territory. Second, you would use the ADX in order to determine whether or not a trend is a strong or weak trend.

It's not necessary to use all the indicators, and when you start researching this you will find that there are a large number of indicators. It's far better to pick out about 3 or at the most 4 and get to know those indicators well. Take the time to study examples of those indicators and read articles about them. Add them to past stock charts and then look at what happened when the indicator behaved in the ways that you're being taught to look for.

You should also spend some time practicing with indicators in real time, before you start making real trades. This will help you develop an ability to read the stock charts along with the indicators to more accurately forecast coming price swings.

Keep in mind that despite all the effort you are going to put into this, you cannot ever attain 100% accuracy. The indicators are not prophets, they are guides. If you view them correctly then you won't be disappointed. It's inevitable that at time all the indicators are pointing in one direction but you still end up with a losing trade. Most of the time they work, but not all the time.

When you are learning your way around stock charts, which you should do before making trades, follow along in real time during the trading day using different indicators. This will help you find the ones that you like best and feel the most comfortable with, and that appear to you to be the best indicators as far as predictability. Practicing will also help you recognize the signals they give in real time. It's one thing to see the data in past history, it's another to recognize it as it's happening.

Something that can be helpful is to buy a small number of shares to practice swing trading in real time. Just buy 3-5 shares at a time of different stocks, and then follow along with your chart patterns and indicators to make buying and selling decisions with some real psychological pressure.

A side note – don't make day trades while doing this. You might find yourself in a panic and making day trades by exiting positions early, the same day that you bought them. This often happens to new traders who tend to panic far more than is really justified. Don't worry if it happens to you, we've all been there.

Conclusion

Start practicing your stock trading skills, stock market analysis, applying different strategies, and using various financial tools, including chart reading. All these are simple and straightforward. If you put your heart and mind to it, you will get to learn and understand how the stock markets function eventually.

It is impressive to learn that buying and selling stocks is a pretty simple affair. Most traders and investors, including novices, can pull this off. The main challenge will be to learn how to choose the winners. There are quite several stocks in all the different industries and sectors of the economy. If you learn how to identify the winning stocks, then you can expect your investments to grow immensely over the years.

A lot of investors across America and elsewhere worldwide have managed to create wealth for themselves and their families through stock market investments. You, too, can achieve this success through prudent trading over time. With different strategies and approaches to stock market investing, if you can find the right approach and be committed to the strategy you choose, you will enjoy long term success. Remember to start investing as soon as possible because the sooner you start, the better off you will be. Investing in the stock market can seem confusing when you are first starting. If you have tried to learn about investing only to find yourself more confused than before, don't feel bad. The abundant information about investing in the stock market can be so complex that it can make trading seem unattainable.

While many people want to overcomplicate investing in the stock market, I have good news for you. None of it is necessary. By investing in index funds and allowing your investment to grow over a long period, you will be able to grow your wealth while avoiding all the overcomplicated information.

Swing trading allows short financial motion in unequivocally slanting stocks to ride the wave toward the example. Swing exchanging merges the best of two universes—the more moderate pace of contributing and the extended potential increments of day exchanging. Swing vendors hold stocks for an impressive period or weeks playing the general upward or plunging designs. Swing Trading isn't fast day exchanging. A couple of individuals call it waves, contributing considering the way that you simply hold puts that are making basic moves. By turning your money over rapidly through transient expands, you can quickly build up your worth.

The basic procedure of swing trading is to dip into an unequivocally inclining stock after its season of company or expiration is done.

A swing trader will most likely make money by getting the quick moves that stocks make in their future and all the while controlling their risk by proper means of the managers' methodologies.

Swing trading joins the best of two universes—the more moderate pace of contributing and the extended potential augmentations of day exchanging.

Swing trading capacities work splendidly for low support vendors—especially those doing it while at work.

While day traders' wager on stocks popping or falling by divisions of centers, swing traders endeavor to ride "swings" in the market. Swing traders buy less shares and go for dynamically basic augmentations, they pay lower business and, theoretically, have an unrivaled probability of gaining progressively immense increments. With day exchanging, the first individual getting rich is the mediator. "Swing vendors go for the meat of the move while a casual investor just gets scraps." Furthermore, to swing exchanging, you don't need refined PC catch ups or lightning smart execution organizations, and you don't have to play entirely erratic stocks.

Swing exchanging is a splendid methodology used by various sellers transversely over various markets. It isn't simply used in the Forex trade, yet it is a crucial mechanical assembly in prospects and financial markets.

Financial experts will, when all is said in done, have a progressively broadened term time horizon and are not generally impacted by fleeting financial changes. Swing exchanging is only a solitary framework and should be used exactly when appropriately grasped. Like any exchanging strategies, swing exchanging can be risky, and a moderate approach can change into day exchanging systems quickly. If you mean to use a swing exchanging system, ensure that you totally appreciate the risks and develop a method that will presumably empower you to create more prominent rate returns on your positions.

Index funds are a great investment for people who don't have the time to go out and learn everything they know about the stock market. You can think of an index fund as a set it and forget it system. When you invest in an index fund, you don't let the market's inevitable fluctuations pull you from your course. Instead, you leave your investment, continue to add to it, and allow it to grow as the market begins to rise again.

By doing this, you will take all the emotions out of investing, and you will be setting yourself up with a nice little nest egg for the future.

With all this insight, you should be able to successfully carry out a trade from start to finish. You must, however, note that the options business is not for every investor.

By now, it is clear to you whether this is an investment you want to try out or not. If you are into it, you must decide the kind of trader you want to be. You can either be a day trader, long term trader, or a short-term trader. As a day trader, you will have the advantage of making several trades that close quickly. This option is good for you if you are interested in making small profits. Otherwise, consider long-term trading that can span over 30 days, but with incredible profits.

Nothing will replace your raw experience when it comes to running this kind of business. As I mentioned before, the best way to gain experience is through experience. The best way to learn how to ride a bike is to work on riding a bike. You must do, and you must try to make progress. The best way to learn how to drive a car is by driving a car.

It is important to note that the shorter the trading period, the higher the stress and risks involved. If you keep holding your trades through the night, you stand a high risk of losing all your capital and destroying your account. Other than this, we are glad that you have learned a new way of earning money from the financial market and understood all the traits and skills you need to make it in binary options trading. Note that theory is never effective without practice.

So, in case you need to get started, it is best to identify a trading platform and put what you have learned into practice. Remember, the more you practice, the more confident you become.

John De Vecchi

- Keep your audiobooks forever, even if you cancel your membership

… and much more

Just scan the QR code below with your smartphone to get started right now FOR FREE!

For Audible US

For Audible UK

For Audible FR

For Audible DE

Author's Note

Thanks for reading my book. If you want to learn more about personal finance, investments, trading, and business, I suggest you follow my author page on Amazon. Through my books, I have decided to share with you the know-how that has allowed me to achieve my financial freedom, to accumulate wealth, and to live the life I want with my family.

My goal is to show you the path for reaching your targets, with useful and applicable information. Only you will be able to tread that path as I did… and now, I'm sharing what I know.

To your wealth!

John De vecchi